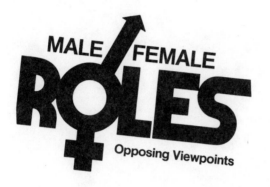

MALE FEMALE

ROLES

Opposing Viewpoints

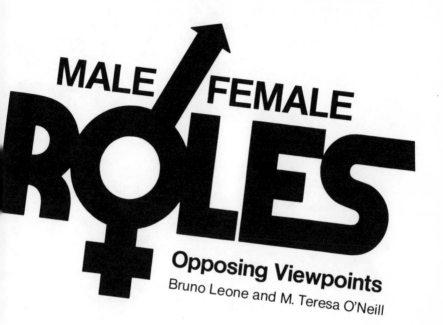

MALE/FEMALE ROLES

Opposing Viewpoints

Bruno Leone and M. Teresa O'Neill

OPPOSING VIEWPOINTS SERIES ®

Greenhaven Press
577 Shoreview Park Road
St. Paul, Minnesota 55112

No part of this book may be reproduced or used in any form or by any means, electrical, mechanical or otherwise, including, but not limited to photocopy, recording or any information storage and retrieval system, without prior written permission from the publisher.

ISBN 0-89908-318-8 Paper Edition
ISBN 0-89908-343-9 Library Edition

"Congress shall make no law . . . abridging the freedom of speech, or of the press.

first amendment to the U.S. Constitution

The basic foundation of our democracy is the first amendment guarantee of freedom of expression. The *Opposing Viewpoints Series* is dedicated to the concept of this basic freedom and the idea that it is more important to practice it than to enshrine it.

Contents

Why Consider Opposing Viewpoints?

"It is better to debate a question without settling it than to settle a question without debating it."

Joseph Joubert (1754-1824)

The Importance of Examining Opposing Viewpoints

The purpose of this book, and the Opposing Viewpoints Series as a whole, is to confront you with alternative points of view on complex and sensitive issues.

Probably the best way to inform yourself is to analyze the positions of those who are regarded as experts and well studied on the issues. It is important to consider every variety of opinion in an attempt to determine the truth. Opinions from the mainstream of society should be examined. Also important are opinions that are considered radical, reactionary, minority or stigmatized by some other uncomplimentary label. An important lesson of history is the fact that many unpopular and even despised opinions eventually gained widespread acceptance. The opinions of Socrates, Jesus and Galileo are good examples of this.

You will approach this book with opinions of your own on the issues debated within it. To have a good grasp of your own viewpoint you must understand the arguments of those with whom you disagree. It is said that those who do not completely understand their adversary's point of view do not fully understand their own.

Perhaps the most persuasive case for considering opposing viewpoints has been presented by John Stuart Mill in his work *On Liberty*. Consider the following statements of his when studying controversial issues:

If all mankind minus one were of one opinion, and only one person were of the contrary opinion, mankind would be no more justified in silencing that one person than he, if he had the power, would be justified in silencing mankind. . . .

We can never be sure that the opinion we are endeavoring to stifle is a false opinion. . . .

All silencing of discussion is an assumption of infallibility. . . .

Ages are no more infallible than individuals; every age having held many opinions which subsequent ages have deemed not only false but absurd; and it is as certain that many opinions now general will be rejected by future ages. . . .

The only way in which a human being can make some approach to knowing the whole of a subject, is by hearing what can be said about it by persons of every variety of opinion, and studying all modes in which it can be looked at by every character of mind. No wise man ever acquired his wisdom in any mode but this.

Pitfalls to Avoid

A pitfall to avoid in considering alternative points of view is that of regarding your own point of view as being merely common sense and the most rational stance, and the point of view of others as being only opinion and naturally wrong. It may be that the opinion of others is correct and that yours is in error.

Another pitfall to avoid is that of closing your mind to the opinions of those whose views differ from yours. The best way to approach a dialogue is to make your primary purpose that of understanding the mind and arguments of the other person and not that of enlightening him or her with your solutions. One learns more by listening than by speaking.

It is my hope that after reading this book you will have a deeper understanding of the issues debated and will appreciate the complexity of even seemingly simple issues when good and honest people disagree. This awareness is particularly important in a democratic society such as ours, where people enter into public debate to determine the common good. People with whom you disagree should not be regarded as enemies, but rather as friends who suggest a different path to a common goal.

Analyzing Sources of Information

The Opposing Viewpoints Series uses diverse sources: magazines, journals, books, newspapers, statements and position papers from a wide range of individuals and organizations. These sources help in the development of a mindset that is open to the consideration of a variety of opinions.

The format of the Opposing Viewpoints Series should help you answer the following questions.

1. Are you aware that three of the most popular weekly news magazines, *Time*, *Newsweek*, and *U.S. News and World Report*, are not totally objective accounts of the news?

2. Do you know there is no such thing as a completely objective author, book, newspaper or magazine?
3. Do you think that because a magazine or newspaper article is unsigned it is always a statement of facts rather than opinions?
4. How can you determine the point of view of newspapers and magazines?
5. When you read do you question an author's frame of reference (political persuasion, training, and life experience)?

Many people finish their formal education unable to cope with these basic questions. They have little chance to understand the social forces and issues surrounding them. Some fall easy victims to demagogues preaching solutions to problems by scapegoating minorities with conspiratorial and paranoid explanations of complex social issues.

I do not want to imply that anything is wrong with authors and publications that have a political slant or bias. All authors have a frame of reference. Readers should understand this. You should also understand that almost all writers have a point of view. An important skill in reading is to be able to locate and identify a point of view. This series gives you practice in both.

Developing Basic Reading and Thinking Skills

A number of basic skills for critical thinking are practiced in the discussion activities that appear throughout the books in the series. Some of the skills are described below.

Evaluating Sources of Information: The ability to choose from among alternative sources the most reliable and accurate source in relation to a given subject.

Distinguishing Between Primary and Secondary Sources: The ability to understand the important distinction between sources which are primary (original or eyewitness accounts) and those which are secondary (historically removed from, and based on, primary sources).

Separating Fact from Opinion: The ability to make the basic distinction between factual statements (those which can be demonstrated or verifed empirically) and statements of opinion (those which are beliefs or attitudes that cannot be proved).

Distinguishing Between Bias and Reason: The ability to differentiate between statements of prejudice (unfavorable, preconceived judgments based on feelings instead of reason) and statements of reason (conclusions that can be clearly and logically explained or justified).

Identifying Stereotypes: The ability to identify oversimplified, exaggerated descriptions (favorable or unfavorable) about people and insulting statements about racial, religious or national groups, based upon misinformation or lack of information.

Recognizing Ethnocentrism: The ability to recognize attitudes or opinions that express the view that one's own race, culture or group is inherently superior, or those attitudes that judge another race,

11

culture, or group in terms of one's own.

It is important to consider opposing viewpoints. It is equally important to be able to critically analyze those viewpoints. The activities in this book will give you practice in mastering these thinking skills. Although the activities are helpful to the solitary reader, they are most useful when the reader can benefit from the interaction of group discussion.

Using this book, and others in the series, will help you develop basic reading and thinking skills. These skills should improve your ability to better understand what you read. You should be better able to separate fact from opinion, substance from rhetoric. You should become a better consumer of information in our media-centered culture.

A Values Orientation

Throughout the Opposing Viewpoints Series you are presented conflicting values. A good example is *American Foreign Policy*. The first chapter debates whether foreign policy should be based on the same kind of moral principles that individuals use in guiding their personal actions, or instead be based primarily on doing what best advances national interests, regardless of moral implications.

The series does not advocate a particular set of values. Quite the contrary! The very nature of the series leaves it to you, the reader, to formulate the values orientation that you find most suitable. My purpose, as editor of the series, is to see that this is made possible by offering a wide range of viewpoints which are fairly presented.

David L. Bender
Opposing Viewpoints Series Editor

Introduction

> "Sexual division has been one of the most basic
> distinctions within society, encouraging one group to
> view its interests differently from another."
>
> Hilda Smith, *Liberating Women's History*

Hilda Smith's comment underscores the fundamental importance of men's and women's attitudes toward one another.
Essential to these attitudes is an individual's sex role, the relationship of a man or woman to society on the basis of gender.
The past twenty years has been witness to the remarkable
changes in traditional male and female roles. Many social
historians mark the onset of these changes and their subsequent
impact on men, women, and families, with the reemergence of
the women's movement. The movement, long a nominal in-
fluence on society and politics, gained broad-based support for
its ideals in the 1960s.

This support, some claim, was generated by an identity crisis
that was recognized simultaneously by millions of women. Betty
Friedan's landmark book *The Feminine Mystique* pinpointed this
widespread discontent: "Fulfillment as a woman had only one
definition for American women after 1949—the housewife-
mother. . . .Her limitless world shrunk to the cozy walls of
home." The new focus on self-fulfillment had a major impact on
men and the family. Barbara Katz in an article for *The National
Observer* sums it up: "For every woman rethinking her
role. . .there's probably a man somewhere rethinking his."

Many men, suddenly confronted with a set of new expectations from women, felt angry, resentful, and lost; others
recognized the limitations of their own traditional male roles and
welcomed the changes. "Men's involvement in breaking out of
the straitjacket of sex roles," wrote Warren Farrell in his book
The Liberated Man, "is essential because of the way it confines
men at the same time it confines women."

Countless relationships between men and women could not
stand the strain of these changes. Divorces increased 301 percent
between 1960 and 1980. The Department of Health and Human
Services estimates that one-third of American children will be af-
fected by divorce by the time they are 18. Some observers interpret these startling statistics as the death knoll of the family.
Others believe that the family is adapting to the new conditions.

Jane Howard in her book *Families* claimed that "Families aren't dying. . . .What families are doing. . .is changing their size and shape and purpose. . . .Only 16.3 percent of this country's 56 million families are conventionally 'nuclear,' with breadwinning fathers, homemaking mothers, and resident children. That leaves 83.7 percent to find other arrangements, which are often so noisy that the clamor resulting is easily mistaken for a death rattle."

This anthology of opposing viewpoints reflects the far-reaching impact of the women's movement on the subject of male/female roles. The questions debated are: How Are Sex Roles Established? Are Women an Oppressed Majority? Do Men Need Liberating? and Is the Family Obsolete? The essential nature of the issues cannot be overstated. When Shakespeare wrote, "All the world's a stage, and all the men and women merely players," he was speaking of the importance of the various roles we play. A major impact on all these roles is how we view ourselves as a woman or a man. And by exploring sex roles we explore much more—we probe the motives, reactions to, and reasons for the way we behave in all interpersonal relationships and in society as a whole.

How Are Sex Roles Established?

"Researchers. . . are finding what they believe is evidence of a genetic component in certain kinds of behavior that have traditionally been identified as masculine or feminine."

Biology Influences Sex Roles

Tim Hackler

Formerly a freelance writer specializing in medicine, Tim Hackler is Arkansas Senator Dale Bumper's press secretary. He continues to write a monthly column for United Airlines' *Mainliner* magazine. A graduate of Columbia University's renowned School of Journalism, Mr. Hackler received his M.A. from Hendrix College in Arkansas in 1971. In the following viewpoint, Mr. Hackler discusses influences on sex differences.

As you read, consider the following questions:
1. According to the author, in what ways do male and female infants differ?
2. According to the studies cited by the author, what accounts for male aggressiveness?
3. How does the author relate the two cerebral hemispheres of the brain to male/female differences?

Reprinted courtesy *United* Magazine, carried aboard *United Airlines.* © 1980. East/West Network, publisher.

Recent research has established beyond a doubt that males and females are born with a different set of "instructions" built into their genetic code. Science is thus confirming what poets and parents have long taken for granted.

Studies at Harvard University and elsewhere show that marked differences between male and female baby behavior are already obvious in the first months of life. Female infants are more oriented toward people. Girls learn to recognize individual human faces and to distinguish between individual voices before male babies of the same age. By four months, a female infant is socially aware enough to distinguish between photographs of familiar people. Girls learn to talk earlier than boys; they articulate better and acquire a more extensive vocabulary than boys of a comparable age. They also begin to smile earlier than boys. (More than one study has found that females continue to smile more than males throughout life.)

Male infants, on the other hand, are more interested in *things*. At four months a boy will react to an inanimate object as readily as to a person. Given the choice between a mother's face and a bright geometric object hanging over his crib, the boy, unlike the girl, will just as frequently babble at the inanimate object as at his mother. A few months later he will begin trying to take it apart. When boys and girls of pre-elementary-school age are asked to manipulate three-dimensional objects, boys overwhelmingly out-perform girls. Boys also show more rough-and-tumble play than girls—as almost any parent can attest—and tend to explore away from their mothers earlier and more often. Stanford psychologists Karl Pribram and Dianne McGuinness conclude that women are "communicative" animals and men are "manipulative" animals.

But to what extent are these sex differences learned, and to what extent are they genetically determined?

Until recently it was widely assumed that most human behavior could be explained by "socialization." In the heredity versus environment argument—sometimes phrased as nature versus nurture—environment was considered of overwhelming importance in determining human behavior. To suggest that any human behavior could even remotely be compared to the instinctive behavior that we see in animals was dismissed as barbarian. Indeed, extreme environmentalists remain committed to the idea that mankind is unlike all other animal species by insisting that heredity has nothing to do with the difference in the ways males and females act and think. If boys and girls were brought up in exactly the same way, they contend, then all behavioral differences between men and women would evaporate.

Biological Connection

This notion has all but collapsed, however, as researchers in both the social and natural sciences are finding what they believe is evidence of a genetic component in certain kinds of behavior—for example, aggression or nurturance—that have traditionally been identified as

17

masculine or feminine.

Of all the behavioral differences between men and women, aggression presents the most clear-cut case for a biological connection. "The evidence cited in favor of genetically based sex differences is more compelling for aggression than for any other temperamental qualities," writes psychologist Janet T. Spence of the University of Texas. Evidence for greater inherent male aggressiveness comes from such diverse sources as ethnology, anthropology, endocrinology, and experimental psychology.

Anatomy or Society?
Little Known Differences Between the Sexes

1. If women who have never given birth are shown a photograph of a baby, the pupils of their eyes expand, indicating pleasure. If men who have never had a child are shown such a photograph, the pupils of their eyes will get smaller.
2. A woman with a very strong sex drive is likely to marry a man who is, overall, a good match for her. A man with a very strong sex drive, however, is likely to concentrate too much on sexual satisfaction and marry someone *not* as well suited.
3. Among right-handed men, the right hemisphere of the brain specializes in visual tasks, the left hemisphere in verbal tasks (and vice versa, to a lesser degree, for left-handed men). Women's brains are not so specialized. This is why a stroke is likely to incapacitate a woman less.
4. Male infants sleep less and are generally more active.
5. Women are faster and more accurate in tasks requiring manual dexterity. That's why so many women are good typists—and why more should be neurosurgeons.
6. Females are more musical; they are, for example, better able to sing in tune. Men who can't tell one note from another outnumber women who can't by 8 to 1.

Adapted from "Little Known Differences Between the Sexes" by Warren Boroson, *NEXT* Magazine, Litton Industries, 1979.

In most animal species, and in all primate species, males are more active, exploratory, and aggressive than females. The primate species, Homo sapiens, is no exception. In no human culture ever studied has the female been found more aggressive than the male. The argument that parents tolerate aggression in boys but discourage it in girls, and that therefore aggression is not genetically determined, but culturally taught does not stand up to recent evidence linking aggression specifically to the male hormone testosterone.

Numerous studies have shown that when testosterone is administered to pregnant laboratory animals, the female offspring show an increase in the incidence of rough-and-tumble play and a decrease in the tendency to withdraw from threats and approaches of other animals.

In a famous decade-long series of studies at Johns Hopkins University, Drs. Anke Ehrhardt and John Money demonstrated that the same phenomenon seemed to be true for human beings as well. They studied girls who had been accidentally exposed prenatally to male hormones and found that these girls considered themselves—and were considered by their mothers—to be more tomboyish than girls in control groups. They showed relatively little interest in dresses and dolls and a greater incidence of rough-and-tumble play. Ehrhardt and Money concluded that the genetically determined presence of male or female sex hormones tends to "wire" the brain for male and female behavior. (It should be emphasized that all of these studies are dealing with the behavior of *average* men and women. We can see that there are many exceptions to the rule....)

Other Differences

If the difference in aggression patterns between the average male and the average female can partially be explained by the effects of genetically determined hormones, what about other differences in the way men and women think and act? We have already seen that one of the most pronounced differences between men and women (a difference already present in the first months of life and continued through adulthood) is that women show verbal superiority, while men show "spatial superiority," a quality that shows up in such tasks as map reading, solving mathematical problems, and perceiving depth.

Researchers have found that this sex difference in skills apparently has something to do with the organization of the brain. It has been known for a decade that the two cerebral hemispheres of the brain are functionally different, and that in the large majority of individuals, the left hemisphere specializes in verbal tasks, while the right hemisphere specializes in spatial perception. It is only recently, however, that neuropsychologists have noticed that males and females differ in their tendencies to use these hemispheres.

Dr. Sandra F. Witelson of McMaster University in Hamilton, Ontario, was among the first to show that males tend to specialize in use of the spatially oriented left hemisphere, while females tend to use their left and right hemispheres about equally, thus implying a relatively greater usage of the linguistically oriented right hemisphere.

Dr. Marylou Reid of the University of Massachusetts has shown that differences in utilization of the hemispheres has already taken place among normal five-year-olds. She concludes: "Since the differences in the sexes are apparent well before puberty, it seems reasonable to suggest that the fetal sex steroids [hormones] may play a critical role in determining relative maturational rates of the two halfbrains and, possibly, of some other bodily regions as well."

Dr. Jerre Levy of the University of Chicago found that girls who had received excessive testosterone prenatally do, as she predicted,

19

show a greater degree of malelike hemispheric specialization than normal females. Furthermore, researchers have identified a sex-linked recessive gene that seems to be associated with high spatial skills and have found that the gene will not be expressed, or "put into effect," without the presence of male hormones.

It bears repeating that all of the sex differences described here represent differences *on the average*. That is to say a minority of women will be found to be more interested in "masculine" pursuits than the average man, and vice versa. Also, there is some evidence that the more creative the individual, the more he or she tends to include both typically male and female behavior in his or her personality. Finally, no experts suggest that the culture in which we live is unimportant in shaping male and female behavior; indeed it is probably more important than genetic considerations.

It does seem certain, however, that the extreme environmental explanation for behavior, which has been so dominant in political and academic thought for the past few decades, is no longer tenable. Males and females may, in fact, be marching to the beat of a different drummer or, as Harvard psychologist Jerome Kagan puts it, they "are sensitized to different aspects of experience and gratified by different profiles of events. . . ."

The most commonly offered explanation for these differences is that such a division of skills had survival value for our ancestors, when men were specialized for skills involved in hunting, and women were specialized for skills involved in rearing children and tending to domestic tasks. (There is some evidence that women may have invented pottery, and it is almost certain that in most cultures they tended to the sewing. This is reflected today in the fact that women are able to perform better at manual dexterity tasks involving fine finger coordination than men.) Even though such division of tasks may have less survival value today than for our ancestors, such specialization has, to some extent, found its way into our genes, since mankind existed in a hunter/gatherer state for the first 99 percent of his history.

"It is clear that parents play a major role in the process of socialization in general and the communication of gender role identity and behavior in particular."

Society Determines Sex Roles

Janet Saltzman Chafetz

Janet Saltzman Chafetz is a feminist and an Associate Professor of Sociology at the University of Houston in Texas. She has contributed to a number of sociological publications. The viewpoint below describes the culturization process that begins at birth and, she believes, determines how individuals will view gender throughout their lives.

As you read, consider the following questions:
1. According to the author, in what ways do parents contribute to sex role identity during a child's infancy?
2. According to David Lynn, what problems does a male child face because he identifies with his mother early in life?
3. Why does the author feel that males are more fearful of and hostile toward homosexuality than females?

Reprinted from *Psychology Today Magazine*. Copyright © 1975, American Psychological Association.

A baby is born knowing nothing, but full of potential. The process by which an individual becomes a creature of society, a socialized human being reflecting culturally defined roles and norms, is complex and as yet imperfectly understood. It is evident, however, that most individuals eventually reflect societal definitions more or less well; most males born and raised in America will someday think and behave like other American males in many important ways and not, for instance, like their Japanese counterparts. Through the socialization process humans come to more or less completely internalize the roles, norms, and values appropriate to the culture and subculture within which they function. Cultural definitions become personal definitions of propriety, normality, and worthiness....

Gender Stamps

The first crucial question asked by the parents of a newborn baby is "What is it? A boy or a girl?" Only later will they be concerned with any other attribute of the infant, even its physical condition; the first priority is to establish its sex. Indeed, almost immediately, gender identity is permanently stamped on the child by the name it is given. Typically, parents have spent long hours mulling over names for a prospective son or daughter months before the birth. They may even have turned to a name glossary for help: here they would find the message that "Boys' and girls' names are, and should be, different. Boys need important names; girls need pretty ones...."

When the proud new father lifts his infant he might jostle it just a little if it's a boy; he will pet and cuddle it if it is a girl. In the months that follow mother will speak to the infant more if it happens to be female—and later everyone will wonder why it is that young girls show greater linguistic skills than boys. Father will continue to play a bit rough with the infant if the child is male. Both parents will discourage a male toddler from "clinging"—but not his sister. Research shows that up to six months of age male infants receive more physical contact from their mothers than do female babies (probably because the male child is valued more), while after that males are more quickly and totally discouraged from such contact.

In one study of 30 new parents it was found that, despite the fact that the boy and girl babies did not differ in physical traits (other than sex), neurological characteristics, or even size, the parents of the girl babies rated them as softer, more finely featured, smaller, and more inattentive than did the parents of boy babies. In general, research shows that parents are more apprehensive about the physical safety of their daughters than their sons. Moreover, parents devote comparatively more attention to teaching their daughters how to smile. And parents soon begin telling little Dick that "big boys don't cry," but the same does not apply to little Jane.

From the beginning of life, the objects that surround an infant, including the clothes in which it is dressed, reflect its sex. Laurel Walum (*The Dynamics of Sex and Gender: A Sociological Perspective*) points out that "there are different styles and colors for male and female babies in such basics as cribs, potty seats, comforters, changing tables, diaper pins, and toys." A trip through any infant and children's store shows that not merely are the colors different, but so are the styles. Often the same basic piece of apparel is designed in two ways: "The male variant snaps from right to left, has a pointed collar and a football motif; the female snaps left to right, has a peter pan collar with lace trim and embroidered butterflies." A little later in life, parents will devote hours to combing *her* hair and putting decorations in it and will bedeck *her* with jewelry, but they will look with horror on *his* games with mother's lipstick or clothes. Jane will often be attired in dresses and told not to get dirty and not to do anything that will let her "underpants show"; Dick will be in trousers with no such restrictions—and later everyone will say that girls are innately less well physically coordinated and weaker than boys. And so begins the life and training of these new human beings.

The description of the early treatment of infants can provide useful insights in terms of the concepts developed above. First, from birth the nature of the interaction between parents and children differs markedly according to the sex of the child. If, indeed, the interaction process is crucial to the development of self-images, it is clear that those of males and females will eventually be quite different. The parents of the little girl relate to her as a breakable object to be carefully tended, protected, and beautified; the little boy's parents treat him as self-reliant, physically active, even "tough," and not very emotionally expressive. These images are undoubtedly learned by the children. In addition, children are verbally instructed and sanctioned for doing or refraining from certain things according to sex. Finally, these restrictions and encouragements serve to "define reality" for children in self-fulfilling ways. If little Jane is assumed to be weak, in need of protection, and an ornamental thing, she will be clothed in apparel reflecting these attributes and informed not to do anything out of keeping with her attire. Unable to swing on the jungle gym and still live up to her parents' image of her and the strictures they impose, she will most certainly fail to develop her muscles; ultimately, she will indeed be weak, in need of protection, and engrossed in her own appearance.

Parent Identification

In taking a closer look at the process by which young children are thought to internalize their gender roles, David Lynn's excellent short text *Parental and Sex Role Identification* (1969) is useful. . . . Lynn begins by asserting that both male and female infants usually establish their initial and principal identification with the mother, an identification that neither sex ever loses entirely. . . . Having established this identity, the female child can continue it and, in so doing, learn the "appropriate" gender role behavior. To the extent that "identification" strongly entails imitation, young Jane need only copy her mother to be rewarded. In this way she quickly begins to internalize the feminine role behavior expected of her.

Little Dick, however, faces a serious problem. Given the relative absence of male figures during his waking hours, the male toddler is hard pressed to find out what he is supposed to do. Early in life his mother begins to sanction him negatively for imitating many of her ways. In this society the father is absent so often the child cannot imitate him, and when he is present, he joins the mother in punishing the boy for being "too feminine." Indeed, he usually surpasses the mother in this, perhaps because of his own gender role insecurities and a resulting fear of homosexuality. The result is that where Jane identifies easily with her mother, Dick must identify with a cultural definition of masculinity that he pieces together from peers, media,

---

Biological Origin

To sum up, role differences developed between the sexes which originally stemmed from physiological differences relating to strength, menstruation, and pregnancy. Then, as social systems developed, these physiological differences and the functional roles that proceeded from them, combined with the actual postures of the two sexes during intercourse, led to a value judgment concerning the dissimilarity of the two sexes, with man seen as superior and woman inferior. In recent centuries, as written language and complex societies came into being, these differences were codified and institutionalized in religion and law, the warp and woof of any social fabric, and if these differences were questioned, the basic fabric of the social system itself became vulnerable. . . .It gradually became apparent, in the view of science at least, that the superiority of the male was no more divinely ordained than the earth was the center of the universe.

Anne Steinmann and David J. Fox, *The Male Dilemma: How to Survive the Sexual Revolution.* New York: Jason Aronson, 1974.

---

a series of don'ts from his parents and so on. In fact, according to Lynn, peers are more important in shaping the identity of males than females. The boy finds out that "boys don't cry," "boys don't cling," and so on, but often on the basis of negative sanctions from parents and peers. Given the lesser efficacy of punishments compared to rewards in the socialization process, it is not surprising that males have greater difficulty establishing their gender role identities than females do. They also fail in this endeavor more frequently, are more anxious about it throughout their lives, and are more hostile toward the other sex. It is also interesting to note that when they become parents, males appear to be more strongly influenced in their behavior and attitudes by the sex of their offspring than do females. This might also reflect insecurity concerning their own gender identity.

The ramifications of this duality are everywhere. Male fear of and hostility toward homosexuality finds little parallel among females, nor does the hang-up of "proving one's masculinity." Girls are far less concerned about the label "tomboy" (and, in fact, often wear it with pride) than boys are about "sissy.". . .

There are other implications of the two rather radically different methods of early gender role learning. Jane, it will be recalled, learns by imitation and positive reinforcement. Dick, on the other hand, has to make a mental effort to comprehend what he is supposed to be, and he more frequently receives negative sanctions. One result, according to Lynn, is that throughout their lives females rely more on affection, or demonstrate a "greater need for affiliation," than males. Males develop greater problem-solving abilities because of this early mental exercise. Moreover, they become more concerned with internalized moral standards than females, who rely more on the opinions of others. . . .

Male Status

In our society males have considerably more prestige, power, and freedom than females. Little children are not oblivious to this fact. Thus, again according to Lynn, although boys experience initially much greater gender role identity problems than girls, as time goes on they become more firmly identified with the masculine role. Females, however, do not do so with reference to the feminine role. Indeed, more girls show preference for the high-prestige and powerful masculine role than boys do for the feminine role, as witnessed by the relative number of "tomboys" and "sissies." Pushing this logic a step further, it is likely that given the higher prestige of the masculine role, homosexuality and sissiness may appear as a kind of betrayal, while lesbianism and tomboyishness may appear as more or less understandable imitations of a superior status role. This would help to explain the far greater social antipathy to the former than the latter. Similarly, feminine fashions often "ape" masculine ones, but the opposite rarely occurs. The whole notion of transvestism basically applies to males only; no one blinks an eye at a female in jeans, a shirt, and boots or sneakers, much less suggests that she is a transvestite, but a male in a skirt (unless he is Scotch or an ancient Roman) is a different matter.

It is clear that parents play a major role in the process of socialization in general and the communication of gender role identity and behavior in particular. Moreover, it is clear that children have established a firm notion of their gender role by about age 3, if not earlier. By this age, little Dick is already objecting to certain things because they are for girls, and Jane is happily imitating mother with her dolls and tea parties.

However, a view of human development that claims that any identities or behavior patterns are irrevocably set for life by that age seems to me to be myopic. Life for most humans *is* change, to a greater or lesser degree. . . . Any such changes away from patterns established

25

by parents must logically be initiated from some source outside the home environment. If society at large provides strong, even coercive supports for identities and behaviors learned early in life from parents, they will be further reinforced rather than changed. This seems, by and large, to be the case with reference to gender roles, inasmuch as most parents reflect stereotypical gender role definitions.

"During the grade-school years, a major job for children is consolidating what it means to be a boy or a girl."

Children Need to Learn Traditional Sex Roles

Kenneth L. Woodward

Kenneth L. Woodward, a graduate of Notre Dame University, is a senior writer and religion editor for *Newsweek Magazine*. He is the winner of several major journalism awards including the 1983 Magazine Award for year-long excellence in religious reporting given by the Religion Public Relations Council. Mr. Woodward is co-author with child psychologist Arthur Kornhaber of *Grandparents/Grandchildren: The Vital Connection*. In the following viewpoint, he reports the concern of child psychiatrists about the de-emphasis on traditional sex roles in childhood.

As you read, consider the following questions:
1. Woodward's article describes the concern of several psychiatrists about the loss of emphasis on traditional sex roles. What effects do they see as a result of this de-emphasis?
2. What motives do these psychiatrists ascribe to the adults who try to eliminate sex roles?
3. Why do the psychiatrists believe that following traditional sex roles is so important?

To child psychiatrist Arthur Kornhaber, the case was disturbingly familiar. At the age of 13, his patient had become a substitute mother in her own home. She did most of the housework and provided most of the care for her younger brother because her working mother hated those chores; her father, raised to do only a man's work in a man's world, refused to help. The teen-ager's problem was not overwork but the crushing shame she felt for actually enjoying the experience of mothering and homemaking that her parents so obviously scorned.

Like many psychiatrists who work with middle-class families, Dr. Kornhaber finds that more and more adolescents are being psychologically sabotaged by adults who really do not want to be parents themselves. "Mothers who don't want to be mothers and 'liberated' women who feel their daughters ought not to learn feminine ways," Kornhaber argues, "are robbing their daughters of their sexual identities. In extreme cases, these kids are being taught at a crucial stage in their development to hate their wombs, their bodies, the whole idea of having and caring for children. And the fathers, by working too much and refusing to share their lives with their sons, are teaching these boys to retreat from their male responsibilities."

Foes

At times, Dr. Kornhaber feels like a voice crying in the wilderness of New York's Westchester County. And well he might. The forces he sees arrayed against sex roles in general and parenting in particular seem formidable: the more militant women's liberationists, for whom mothering is a form of indentured servitude; overachieving fathers, for whom inflation is a goad to still longer hours at work; and an increasingly androgynous youth culture that seeks psychological security by deliberately blurring sexual distinctions. What it all adds up to is an assault on Sigmund Freud and his assumption that biological nature sets certain limits to male and female sexual identity—without which there would be no human beings at all. The American middle-class family, with its increasing individualism and sexual egalitarianism, seems bent on proving that Father Freud was wrong.

"One of the most startling things I've seen among today's affluent adolescents is the slurring of gender," says Dr. Ralph Greenson, who was Marilyn Monroe's psychiatrist back in the days when some women could become unambiguous sex symbols. "I have the impression that girls and boys are looking for twins, rather than lovers." As examples of adolescent gender-confusion, Dr. Greenson cites the increasing promiscuity among girls aged 13 and 14, who "talk about 'balling' the way boys used to, except they *do* it. I think this is taking on a masculine attitude picked up from older boys." Among boys the same age, the Beverly Hills psychiatrist finds "an enormous increase in passivity" marked by a refusal to work and an assumption that "masculinity is equated with killing."

Not surprisingly, child psychiatrists are themselves deeply divided over how they should react to these shifting sexual boundaries among

28

American adolescents. "Teaching little girls how to cook and to sew just won't wash with kids in our mobile middle classes," says child psychoanalyst Paul Adams of Miami, Fla. "It's just as well. The woman's movement, the gay movement, all these liberation movements have caught psychiatrists off guard. We were too busy adjusting people to the sex roles defined by the cultural status quo."

Sexual Integration

It is of very doubtful value to enlist the gifts of women if bringing women into fields that have been defined as male frightens the men, unsexes the women, muffles and distorts the contribution women could make.

Margaret Mead, *Male and Female*, 1948.

Some psychiatrists argue that the status quo itself should be abolished. In a paper on "Conceptions of Sex Role," Jeanne Humphrey Block argues that adults raised to assume traditional sex roles are less satisfied with themselves than those allowed to assume broader sexual identities. Block believes that "sexual identity means, or will mean, the earning of a sense of self" that will allow individuals to manifest "human qualities which our society, until now, has labeled unwomanly or unmanly." Thus, in her view, aggressive women and passive men need not feel like sexual misfits.

Learning Sex Roles

The conflict over appropriate sex roles runs into unresolved questions of what sexual identity is and how it is formed. According to most psychologists, sexual identity is built up by stages beginning with genes, hormones, early mothering and family upbringing. In these early years, parents may give dolls to boys or baseball mitts to girls, so long as their intent is not to destroy the child's basic biological identity.

Once children begin to spend time outside the home, however, some psychiatrists feel that traditional sex roles become more important. "During the grade-school years, a major job for children is consolidating what it means to be a boy or a girl," says child psychiatrist Thomas Johnson of San Diego. "This is done partly by identification with children of the same sex," Johnson argues. Same-sex organizations such as the Little League and the Campfire Girls, he believes, allow children the necessary freedom to discuss with their peers the sexual changes going on inside them. Unfortunately, says Dr. Johnson, "I'm seeing more and more children concerned and confused with sexual roles," a situation he feels is aggravated by "some in the women's liberation movement who would do away with recognizing any differences between boys and girls."

The real war over sex roles, however, is now being waged in the early stages of adolescence. To some psychiatrists like Dr. Kornhaber, who spend most of their time in therapy with disturbed adolescents, the learning of traditional sex roles is a necessary step in completing a child's sexual identity. "Mothering and fathering are trans-cultural roles, rooted in biology and anatomy," he argues. "So long as mothers and fathers are needed, adolescents must learn from their same-sex parent to anticipate—with pleasure—these basic human experiences. Later on, boys and girls may want to modify their sex roles, but they should first learn these nurturing skills, and not be robbed of them by liberated parents who may simply be on an adult head trip."

Learning to Care

Few psychiatrists are such strict sexual constructionists. But there are many who concede that adolescents who are not shown how to be properly nurturing mothers and fathers will emerge into adulthood unable to give or receive any kind of human warmth. With this in mind, the U.S. Office of Child Development and the Office of Education last year sponsored programs in which teen-age girls and boys from some 234 school districts were taken into daycare and nursery centers to learn how to care for infants. "Youngsters should learn how to be parents," says W. Stanley Kruger, special programs director at USOE, "and those who do not want to become parents should have enough information to make a sound choice."

The question remains whether mothering and fathering can really be learned outside an intimate family environment. And there is a question, too, whether sexual identity is complete without some kind of experience of parenthood itself. In their efforts to help patients adjust to the American cultural "norm," some psychotherapists may undoubtedly throw Freud aside. But other observers wonder whether middle-class America hasn't gone too far in ignoring nature and nurture. In an essay on Freud, anthropologist Margaret Mead observes that "the path he outlined . . . still suggests that the rhythms of human development, patterned during a million years, are ignored at our peril, and understood give us wisdom." But it appears to be the fashion these days to disrupt all inherited patterns and to defy in a million small ways what nature seems bent on preserving.

"I have come to believe that we need a new standard of psychological health for the sexes, one that removes the burden of stereotype and allows people to feel free to express the best traits of men and women."

Traditional Sex Roles Are Too Restrictive

Sandra Lipsitz Bem

A professor of psychology at Cornell University, Sandra Lipsitz Bem has done extensive study on the consequences of traditional sex roles. The following viewpoint expresses her views, reinforced by her research, of the importance of androgeny. Androgeny can be described as the replacement of traditional gender stereotypes by impartial receptivity to the skills, interests and talents of individuals regardless of their gender.

As you read, consider the following questions:

1. What does "androgynous" mean? Why does Dr. Bem think that this is the ideal way for people to be?
2. What evidence does Dr. Bem cite to show that traditional sex roles are psychologically harmful to men and women?
3. What evidence does she cite to show that these roles are, at the very least, restrictive?

In American society, men are supposed to be masculine, women are supposed to be feminine, and neither sex is supposed to be much like the other. If men are independent, tough and assertive, women should be dependent, sweet and retiring. A womanly woman may be tender and nurturant, but no manly man may be so.

For years we have taken these polar opposites as evidence of psychological health. Even our psychological tests of masculinity and femininity reflect this bias: a person scores as *either* masculine *or* feminine, but the tests do not allow a person to say that he or she is both.

I have come to believe that we need a new standard of psychological health for the sexes, one that removes the burden of stereotype and allows people to feel free to express the best traits of men and women. As many feminists have argued, freeing people from rigid sex roles and allowing them to be *androgynous* (from "andro," male, and "gyne," female), should make them more flexible in meeting new situations, and less restricted in what they can do and how they can express themselves.

In fact, there is already considerable evidence that traditional sex typing is unhealthy. For example, high femininity in females consistently correlates with high anxiety, low self-esteem, and low self-acceptance. And although high masculinity in males has been related to better psychological adjustment during adolescence, it is often accompanied during adulthood by high anxiety, high neuroticism, and low self-acceptance. Further, greater intellectual development has quite consistently correlated with cross-sex typing (masculinity in girls, femininity in boys). Boys who are strongly masculine and girls who are strongly feminine tend to have lower overall intelligence, lower spatial ability, and show lower creativity.

In addition, it seems to me that traditional sex typing necessarily restricts behavior. Because people learn, during their formative years, to suppress any behavior that might be considered undesirable or inappropriate for their sex, men are afraid to do "women's work," and women are afraid to enter "man's world." Men are reluctant to be gentle, and women to be assertive. In contrast, androgynous people are not limited by labels. They are able to do whatever they want, both in their behavior and their feelings.

Measuring Androgeny

I decided to study this question, to see whether sex-typed people really were more restricted and androgynous people more adaptable. Because I needed a way to measure how masculine, feminine, or androgynous a person was, I developed the Bem Sex Role Inventory (BSRI), which consists of a list of 60 personality characteristics: 20 traditionally masculine (ambitious, self-reliant, independent, assertive); 20 traditionally feminine (affectionate, gentle, understanding, sensitive to the needs of others); and 20 neutral (truthful, friendly, likable) . . . .

32

Kate Salley Palmer, *The Greenville News.* Reprinted with permission.

My colleagues and I have given the BSRI to more than 1,500 undergraduates at Stanford University. Semester after semester, we find that about 50 percent of the students adhere to "appropriate" sex roles, about 15 percent are cross sex typed, and about 35 percent are androgynous.

With the BSRI in hand, we were in a position to find out whether sex typed people really were restricted and androgynous people really more adaptable. Our strategy was to measure a number of behaviors that were stereotypically either masculine or feminine. We selected these particular actions to represent the very best of what masculinity and femininity have come to stand for, and we felt that any healthy adult should be capable of them. We predicted that sex-typed people would do well only when the behavior was traditionally considered appropriate for his or her sex, whereas those who were androgynous would do well regardless of the sex-role stereotype attached to the particular action.

The masculine behaviors that we selected were independence and assertiveness....

The feminine behaviors that we selected all measured the extent to which a person was willing to be responsible for or helpful toward another living creature....

Restrictive Sex Roles

The pattern of results for these five experiments suggests that rigid sex roles can seriously restrict behavior. This is especially the case for men. The masculine men did masculine things very well, but they did not do feminine things. They were independent and assertive when they needed to be, but they...lacked the ability to express warmth, playfulness and concern, important human—if traditionally feminine—traits.

Similarly, the feminine women were restricted in their ability to express masculine characteristics. They did feminine things...but they weren't independent in judgment or assertive of their own preferences....

In contrast, the androgynous men and women did just about everything. They could be independent and assertive when they needed to be, and warm and responsive in appropriate situations. It didn't matter, in other words, whether a behavior was stereotypically masculine or feminine; they did equally well on both....

We went one step further, because we wondered how sex-typed people would feel about themselves if they *had* to carry out an opposite-sex activity. We asked all the students to perform three masculine, three feminine, and three neutral activities while we photographed them, and then they indicated on a series of scales how each activity made them feel about themselves. Masculine men and feminine women felt much worse than androgynous people about doing a cross-sex task. Traditional men felt less masculine if they had to, say, prepare a baby bottle and traditional women felt less feminine if they had to nail boards together. When the experimenter was a member of the opposite sex, sex-typed students were especially upset about acting out of role. They felt less attractive and likeable, more nervous and peculiar, less masculine or feminine, and didn't particularly enjoy the experience.

This research persuades me that traditional concepts of masculinity and femininity do restrict a person's behavior in important ways. In a modern complex society like ours, an adult has to be assertive, independent and self-reliant, but traditional femininity makes many women unable to behave in these ways. On the other hand, an adult must also be able to relate to other people, to be sensitive to their needs and concerned about their welfare, as well as to be able to depend on them for emotional support. But traditional masculinity keeps men from responding in such supposedly feminine ways.

Androgyny, in contrast, allows an individual to be both independent and tender, assertive and yielding, masculine and feminine. Thus androgyny greatly expands the range of behavior open to everyone, permitting people to cope more effectively with diverse situations. As such, I hope that androgyny will some day come to define a new and more human standard of psychological health.

Distinguishing Primary from Secondary Sources

A critical thinker must always question his or her source of knowledge. One way to critically evaluate information is to be able to distinguish between *primary sources* (a "firsthand" or eyewitness account from personal letters, documents, or speeches, etc.) and *secondary sources* (a "secondhand" account usually based upon a "firsthand" account and possibly appearing in newspapers, encyclopedias, or other similar types of publications). A diary about the Civil War written by a Civil War veteran is an example of a primary source. A history of the Civil War written many years after the war and relying, in part, upon that diary for information is an example of a secondary source.

However, it must be noted that interpretation and/or point of view also play a role when dealing with primary and secondary sources. For example, the historian writing about the Civil War not only will quote from the veteran's diary but also will interpret it. It is certainly a possibility that his or her interpretation may be incorrect. Even the diary of primary source must be questioned as to interpretation and point of view. The veteran may have been a militarist who stressed the glory of warfare rather than the human suffering involved.

This activity is designed to test your skill in evaluating sources of information. Pretend that you are writing a research paper on the origins of sex roles. You decide to include an equal number of primary and secondary sources. Listed below are a number of sources which may be useful in your research. Carefully evaluate each of them. First, place a *P* next to those descriptions you feel would serve as primary sources. Second, rank the primary sources assigning the number (1) to the most objective and accurate primary sources, number (2) to the next accurate and so on until the ranking is finished. Repeat the entire procedure, this time placing an *S* next to those descriptions you feel would serve as secondary sources and then ranking them.

If you are doing this activity as a member of a class or group, discuss and compare your evaluation with other members of the group. If you are reading this book alone, you may want to ask others if they agree with your evaluation. Either way, you will find the interaction very valuable.

P or S

_____ 1. A report in *Newsweek* magazine dealing with the
research currently being done about sex roles. _____

_____ 2. A novel by a sociologist set in prehistoric times and
showing male and female characters developing in different ways because of the conditions of their world
and the demands of their tribe. _____

_____ 3. A report about sex role development by anthropologist
Margaret Mead who observed and lived with several
primitive groups of people over a period of 14 years. _____

_____ 4. Two autobiographies—one by a man, one by a
woman—each detailing the influences that led them to
their perceptions of themselves and their gender roles. _____

_____ 5. A report by a pair of psychologists describing the
results of controlled behavioral experiments they have
done over a period of several years to determine how
gender roles are established. _____

_____ 6. A report by a scientist describing the sex role effects of
her hormone experiments on monkeys. _____

_____ 7. A documentary film about sex role researcher John
Money and his methods. _____

_____ 8. A newspaper report of a speech made by a scientist in
which he described the results of his research into the
differences between male and female brains. _____

_____ 9. A minister's sermon about male and female roles as
established by God and set down in the Bible. _____

_____ 10. A book by an anthropologist in which she interprets
evidence and artifacts from ancient cultures in light of
what they imply about sex roles. _____

_____ 11. A book by a psychiatrist explaining sex role origins as
described by Sigmund Freud in his journals. _____

_____ 12. The transcript of an interview between a journalist
and a sex role researcher in which the researcher
discusses the conclusions he has drawn during his
several years of work on this subject. _____

Bibliography

The following list of periodical articles deals with the subject matter of this chapter.

Jerry Adler with Gerald C. Lubenow	"Cavewoman's New Image," *Newsweek*, November 23, 1981.
John W. Alexander	"Headship in Marriage: Flip of a Coin?" *Christianity Today*, February 20, 1981.
T.B. Brazelton	"Should We Treat Our Son and Daughter Just Alike?" *Redbook*, August 1980.
James R. Edwards	"Toward a Neutered Bible: Making God S/He," *Christianity Today*, February 18, 1983.
Paul Handy Furfey	"Was St. Paul a Closet Feminist?" *U.S. Catholic*, May 1980.
David Gelman & Others	"Just How the Sexes Differ," *Newsweek*, May 18, 1981.
Carol Gilligan	"Why Should a Woman Be More Like a Man?" *Psychology Today*, June 1982.
Daniel Goleman	"Special Abilities of the Sexes: Do They Begin in the Brain?" *Psychology Today*, November 1978.
Vivian Gornick	"Watch Out: Your Brain May Be Used Against You," *Ms.*, April 1982.
Annie Gottlieb	"Men and Women: What Difference Do the Differences Really Make?" *Mademoiselle*, July 1981.
Judith B. Hooper	"Feminism and the Brain," *Omni*, July 1981.
Wista Johnson	"Do We Raise Our Sons to Be Sexist?" *Essense*, November 1982.
Diane McGuinness	"How Schools Discriminate Against Boys," *Human Nature*, February 1979.
Mary Brown Parlee	"The Sexes Under Scrutiny: From Old Biases to New Theories," *Psychology Today*, November 1978.
Joseph H. Pleck	"Prisoners of Manliness," *Psychology Today*, September 1981.
Lettie C. Pogrebin	"Getting Along in a Nonsexist Family," *Ms.*, October 1980.
J.E. Poznik	"Little Boy Lib," *Parents*, October 1981.
Martin Safer	"Women's Ambidextrous Brains," *Psychology Today*, March 1982.
Peggy J. Schmidt	"Sexist Schooling," *Working Woman*, October 1982.
Miriam Schneir	"New Jobs for Men," *McCall's*, August 1981.

Science Digest	"Linking Sex With Learning," March 1982.
Science Digest	"M/F Thought Processes—How They Differ," March 1980.
Martin Simmons	"Relationships in the Eighties: Going Through Changes," *Essense*, September 1982.
Janet Spector	"When Sexism Was Born," *USA Today*, February 1981.
Donald Symons interviews Sam Keen	"Eros and Alley Oop," *Psychology Today*, April 1983.
Carol Tavris	"How Would Life Be Different if You'd Been Born a Boy?" *Redbook*, February 1983.
Carol Tavris	"The Meaning of Sex Ratios," *Psychology Today*, April 1983.
Judith Thurman interviews Nancy Chodorow	"Breaking the Mother-Daughter Code," *Ms.*, September 1982.
U.S. News & World Report	"As Men Move in on Women's Jobs," August 10, 1981.
Judith Viorst	"Are Men and Women Different?" *Redbook*, November 1978.
E.O. Wilson	"Sex Role Differences: Why?...And Their Future Importance?" *Science Digest*, February 1980.

CHAPTER 2

Are Women an Oppressed Majority?

"In the feminine mystique, there is no other way for a woman to dream. . .about herself, except as her children's mother, her husband's wife."

Tradition Oppresses Women

Betty Friedan

Betty Friedan, one of America's foremost spokeswomen for women's rights, is a writer, teacher, parent and activist for such issues as abortion reform and the Equal Rights Amendment. Her most recent book, *The Second Stage* (1982), points out women's need for family as well as for individual identities. Ms. Friedan's 1963 book, *The Feminine Mystique,* was the catalyst for the women's movement—the work that inspired and united women all over the country in their efforts to strive for equality of opportunity with men. The following viewpoint, from that book, describes what she called the feminine mystique and the basic problems it creates.

As you read, consider the following questions:
1. According to Ms. Friedan, how did the media image of women change from the 1930s to the late 1940s?
2. What *is* the "feminine mystique"?
3. What is the basic problem with this mystique, according to Ms. Friedan?

Reprinted from *The Feminine Mystique* by Betty Friedan, by permission of W.W. Norton & Company, Inc. Copyright © 1974, 1963 by Betty Friedan.

In 1939, the heroines of women's magazine stories were not always young, but in a certain sense they were younger than their fictional counterparts today. They were young in the same way that the American hero has always been young: they were New Women, creating with a gay determined spirit a new identity for women—a life of their own. There was an aura about them of becoming, of moving into a future that was going to be different from the past. The majority of heroines in the four major women's magazines (then *Ladies' Home Journal, McCall's, Good Housekeeping, Woman's Home Companion*) were career women—happily, proudly, adventurously, attractively career women—who loved and were loved by men. And the spirit, courage, independence, determination—the strength of character they showed in their work as nurses, teachers, artists, actresses, copywriters, saleswomen—were part of their charm. There was a definite aura that their individuality was something to be admired, not unattractive to men, that men were drawn to them as much for their spirit and character as for their looks. . . .

Occupation: Housewife

And then suddenly the image blurs. The New Woman, soaring free, hesitates in midflight, shivers in all that blue sunlight and rushes back to the cozy walls of home. [In 1949], the *Ladies' Home Journal* printed the prototype of the innumerable paeans to "Occupation: Housewife" that started to appear in the women's magazines, paeans that resounded throughout the fifties. They usually begin with a woman complaining that when she has to write "housewife" on the census blank, she gets an inferiority complex. ("When I write I realize that here I am, a middle-aged woman, with a university education, and I've never made anything out of my life. I'm just a housewife.") Then the author of the paean, who somehow never is a housewife (in this case, Dorothy Thompson, newspaper woman, foreign correspondent, famous columnist, in *Ladies' Home Journal*, March 1949), roars with laughter. The trouble with you, she scolds, is you don't realize you are expert in a dozen careers, simultaneously. "You might write: business manager, cook, nurse, chauffeur, dressmaker, interior decorator, accountant, caterer, teacher, private secretary—or just put down philanthropist. . . . All your life you have been giving away your energies, your skills, your talents, your services, for love." . . .

As for not earning any money, the argument goes, let the housewife compute the cost of her services. Women can save more money by their managerial talents inside the home than they can bring into it by outside work. As for woman's spirit being broken by the boredom of household tasks, maybe the genius of some women has been thwarted, but a "world full of feminine genius, but poor in children, would come rapidly to an end. . . . Great men have great mothers." . . .

The Feminine Mystique

And so the feminine mystique began to spread through the land. . . .

The feminine mystique says that the highest value and the only commitment for women is the fulfillment of their own femininity. It says that the great mistake of Western culture, through most of its history, has been the undervaluation of this femininity. It says this femininity is so mysterious and intuitive and close to the creation and origin of life that man-made science may never be able to understand it. But however special and different, it is in no way inferior to the nature of man; it may even in certain respects be superior. The mistake, says the mystique, the root of women's troubles in the past is that women envied men, women tried to be like men, instead of accepting their own nature, which can find fulfillment only in sexual passivity, male domination, and nurturing maternal love.

Choosing a Value System

All my life I have wanted to be a homemaker and mother, and I was so afraid that feminism was a threat to these beliefs. Instead the beliefs I once held because of cultural influences are based on intense conviction. . . .I have recognized the inequities that are dealt the homemaker under the law, and the lack of real respect that the homemaker receives from all areas of society, and have been moved to fight for greater recognition of her contribution. In doing so, I have come to believe in the value of the traditional roles of women more than ever. It is a masculine. . . value system which says that earning money and making it in the business world is what is important. As a feminist, I value the nurturing and the caring that women have traditionally done as infinitely worthwhile. It becomes particularly meaningful when it's something that women choose as equals rather than have imposed upon them as inferiors.

Anne Bowen Follis, *I'm Not a Women's Libber,But. . .* New York: Avon, 1982.

But the new image this mystique gives to American women is the old image: "Occupation: housewife." The new mystique makes the housewife-mothers, who never had a chance to be anything else, the model for all women; it presupposes that history has reached a final and glorious end in the here and now, as far as women are concerned. Beneath the sophisticated trappings, it simply makes certain concrete, finite, domestic aspects of feminine existence—as it was lived by women whose lives were confined, by necessity, to cooking, cleaning, washing, bearing children—into a religion, a pattern by which all women must now live or deny their femininity.

Problems Redefined

Fulfillment as a woman had only one definition for American women after 1949—the housewife-mother. . . .

Thus the logic of the feminine mystique redefined the very nature of woman's problem. When woman was seen as a human being of limitless human potential, equal to man, anything that kept her from realizing her full potential was a problem to be solved: barriers to higher education and political participation, discrimination or prejudice in law or morality. But now that woman is seen only in terms of her sexual role, the barriers to the realization of her full potential, the prejudices which deny her full participation in the world, are no longer problems. The only problems now are those that might disturb her adjustment as a housewife. So career is a problem, education is a problem, political interest, even the very admission of women's intelligence and individuality is a problem. And finally there is the problem that has no name, a vague undefined wish for "something more" than washing dishes, ironing, punishing and praising the children. . . .

Over and over again, stories in women's magazines insist that woman can know fulfillment only at the moment of giving birth to a child. They deny the years when she can no longer look forward to giving birth, even if she repeats that act over and over again. In the feminine mystique, there is no other way for a woman to dream of creation or of the future. There is no way she can even dream about herself, except as her children's mother, her husband's wife. And the documentary articles play back new young housewives, grown up under the mystique, who do not have even that "question within myself." Says one, described in "How America Lives" (*Ladies' Home Journal*, June, 1959): "If he doesn't want me to wear a certain color or a certain kind of dress, then I truly don't want to, either. The thing is, whatever he has wanted is what I also want. . . . I don't believe in fifty-fifty marriages." . . .

There is no problem, in the logic of the feminine mystique, for such a woman who has no wishes of her own, who defines herself only as wife and mother. . . .

Staring uneasily at this image, I wonder if a few problems are not somehow better than this smiling empty passivity. If they are happy, these young women who live the feminine mystique, then is this the end of the road? Or are the seeds of something worse than frustration inherent in this image? Is there a growing divergence between this image of woman and human reality? . . .

A Question of Identity

What happens when women try to live according to an image that makes them deny their minds? What happens when women grow up in an image that makes them deny the reality of the changing world?

The material details of life, the daily burden of cooking and cleaning, of taking care of the physical needs of husband and children—these did indeed define a woman's world a century ago when Americans were pioneers, and the American frontier lay in conquering the land. But the women who went west with the wagon trains also shared the pioneering purpose. Now the American frontiers are of the mind and of the spirit. Love and children and home are good, but they are not the whole world. . . . Why should women accept this

44

picture of a half-life, instead of a share in the whole of human destiny? Why should women try to make housework "something more," instead of moving on the frontiers of their own time, as American women moved beside their husbands on the old frontiers?

A baked potato is not as big as the world, and vacuuming the living room floor—with or without makeup—is not work that takes enough thought or energy to challenge any woman's full capacity. Women are human beings, not stuffed dolls, not animals....

Don Wright, *Miami News*. Reprinted with permission.

The feminine mystique permits, even encourages, women to ignore the question of their identity. The mystique says they can answer the question "Who am I?" by saying "Tom's wife... Mary's mother."...

It is my thesis that the core of the problem for women today is not sexual but a problem of identity—a stunting or evasion of growth that is perpetuated by the feminine mystique. It is my thesis that as the Victorian culture did not permit women to accept or gratify their basic sexual needs, our culture does not permit women to accept or gratify their basic need to grow and fulfill their potentialities as human beings, a need which is not solely defined by their sexual role....

For the first time in their history, women are becoming aware of an identity crisis in their own lives, a crisis which began many generations ago, has grown worse with each succeeding generation, and will not end until they, or their daughters, turn an unknown corner and make of themselves and their lives the new image that so many women now so desperately need.

In a sense that goes beyond any one woman's life, I think this is the crisis of women growing up—a turning point from an immaturity that has been called femininity to full human identity. I think women had to suffer this crisis of identity, which began a hundred years ago, and have to suffer it still today, simply to become fully human.

"Fulfillment for most women involves expressing their natural maternal urge by loving and caring for someone."

Tradition Uplifts Women

Phyllis Schlafly

Phyllis Schlafly, a highly energetic, conservative political activist, graduated from Washington University in St. Louis, Missouri. She earned a Master's Degree from Radcliffe in one year and later earned a law degree from Washington University. She is best known for her extremely effective campaign against the Equal Rights Amendment. In this viewpoint, Mrs. Schlafly discusses the differences between women liberationists and what she terms the positive woman, the woman who is proud of her difference from men and who uses her womanliness to enhance her life and the lives of those around her.

As you read, consider the following questions:
1. What objections does Mrs. Schlafly have to the women's libera-tion movement?
2. Mrs. Schlafly describes at length the physical differences between men and women. Why do you think she puts so much emphasis on this?
3. What mental (psychological and philosophical) differences between men and women does Mrs. Schlafly describe? What, according to her, is the significance of these differences?

The first requirement for the acquisition of power by the Positive Woman is to understand the differences between men and women. Your outlook on life, your faith, your behavior, your potential for fulfillment, all are determined by the parameters of your original premise. The Positive Woman starts with the assumption that the world is her oyster. She rejoices in the creative capability within her body and the power potential of her mind and spirit. She understands that men and women are different, and that those very differences provide the key to her success as a person and fulfillment as a woman.

The women's liberationist, on the other hand, is imprisoned by her own negative view of herself and of her place in the world around her. This view of women was most succinctly expressed in an advertisement designed by the principal woman's liberationist organization, the National Organization for Women (NOW), and run in many magazines and newspapers and as spot announcements on many television stations. The advertisement showed a darling curlyheaded girl with the caption: "This healthy, normal baby has a handicap. She was born female."

This is the self-articulated dog-in-the-manger, chip-on-the-shoulder, fundamental dogma of the women's liberation movement. Someone—it is not clear who, perhaps God, perhaps the "Establishment," perhaps a conspiracy of male chauvinist pigs—dealt women a foul blow by making them female. It becomes necessary, therefore, for women to agitate and demonstrate and hurl demands on society in order to wrest from an oppressive male-dominated social structure the status that has been wrongfully denied to women through the centuries.

By its very nature, therefore, the women's liberation movement precipitates a series of conflict situations—in the legislatures, in the courts, in the schools, in industry—with man targeted as the enemy. Confrontation replaces cooperation as the watchword of all relationships. Women and men become adversaries instead of partners.

The second dogma of the women's liberationists is that, of all the injustices perpetrated upon women through the centuries, the most oppressive is the cruel fact that women have babies and men do not. Within the confines of the women's liberationist ideology, therefore, the abolition of this overriding inequality of women becomes the primary goal. . . .

Women must be made equal to men in their ability *not* to become pregnant and *not* to be expected to care for babies they may bring into the world. . . .

The Positive Woman will never travel that dead-end road. It is self-evident to the Positive Woman that the female body with its baby-producing organs was not designed by a conspiracy of men but by the Divine Architect of the human race. . . .

The Positive Woman looks upon her femaleness and her fertility as part of her purpose, her potential, and her power. She rejoices that she has a capability for creativity that men can never have.

The third basic dogma of the women's liberation movement is that there is no difference between male and female except the sex organs, and that those physical, cognitive, and emotional differences you *think* are there, are merely the result of centuries of restraints imposed by a male-dominated society and sex-stereotyped schooling. The role imposed on women is, by definition, inferior, according to the women's liberationists.

Male/Female Competition

The Positive Woman knows that, while there are some physical competitions in which women are better (and can command more money) than men, including those that put a premium on grace and beauty, such as figure skating, the superior physical strength of males over females in competitions of strength, speed, and short-term endurance is beyond rational dispute . . . .

Nick, *Punch*   Rothco

"Serves her right. She was always whining about women not being allowed to participate in the services."

Nick. © Punch/Rothco. Reprinted with permission.

The women's liberationists are expending their time and energies erecting a make-believe world in which they hypothesize that *if* schooling were gender-free, and *if* the same money were spent on male and female sports programs, and *if* women were permitted to compete on equal terms, *then* they would prove themselves to be physically equal. Meanwhile, the Positive Woman has put the ineradicable physical differences into her mental computer, programmed her plan of action, and is already on the way to personal achievement.

Thus, while some militant women spend their time demanding more money for professional sports, ice skater Janet Lynn, a truly Positive Woman, quietly signed the most profitable financial contract in the history of women's athletics. It was not the strident demands of the women's liberationists that brought high prices to women's tennis, but the discovery by sports promoters that beautiful female legs gracefully moving around the court made women's tennis a highly marketable television production to delight male audiences. . . .

Despite the claims of the women's liberation movement, there are countless physical differences between men and women. The female body is 50 to 60 percent water, the male 60 to 70 percent water, which explains why males can dilute alcohol better than women and delay its effect. The average woman is about 25 percent fatty tissue, while the male is 15 percent, making women more buoyant in water and able to swim with less effort. Males have a tendency to color blindness. Only 5 percent of persons who get gout are female. Boys are born bigger. Women live longer in most countries of the world, not only in the United States where we have a hard-driving competitive pace. Women excel in manual dexterity, verbal skills, and memory recall. . .

Does the physical advantage of men doom women to a life of servility and subservience? The Positive Woman knows that she has a complementary advantage which is at least as great—and, in the hands of a skillful woman, far greater. The Divine Architect who gave men a superior strength to lift weights also gave women a different kind of superior strength. . . .

A Positive Woman cannot defeat a man in a wrestling or boxing match, but she can motivate him, inspire him, encourage him, teach him, restrain him, reward him, and have power over him that he can never achieve over her with all his muscle. How or whether a Positive Woman uses her power is determined solely by the way she alone defines her goals and develops her skills.

Woman's Strength

The differences between men and women are also emotional and psychological. Without woman's innate maternal instinct, the human race would have died out centuries ago. There is nothing so helpless in all earthly life as the newborn infant. It will die within hours if not cared for. Even in the most primitive, uneducated societies, women have always cared for their newborn babies. They didn't need any schooling to teach them how. They didn't need any welfare workers to tell them it is their social obligation. Even in societies to whom such concepts as "ought," "social responsibility," and "compassion for the helpless" were unknown, mothers cared for their new babies.

Why? Because caring for a baby serves the natural maternal need of a woman. Although not nearly so total as the baby's need, the woman's need is nonetheless real.

The overriding psychological need of a woman is to love something alive. A baby fulfills this need in the lives of most women. If a baby is not available to fill that need, women search for a baby-substitute. This is the reason why women have traditionally gone into teaching and nursing careers. They are doing what comes naturally to the female psyche. The schoolchild or the patient of any age provides an outlet for a woman to express her natural maternal need. . . .

The women's liberation movement complains that traditional stereotyped roles assume that women are "passive" and that men are "aggressive." The anomaly is that a woman's most fundamental emotional need is not passive at all, but active. A woman naturally seeks to love affirmatively and to show that love in an active way by caring for the object of her affections. . . .

Women Are Women

It would be futile to attempt to fit women into a masculine pattern of attitudes, skills, abilities and disastrous to force them to suppress their specifically female characteristics and abilities by keeping up the pretense that there are no differences between the sexes.

Arianna Stassinopoulos, *The Female Woman,* 1973.

Finally, women are different from men in dealing with the fundamentals of life itself. Men are philosophers, women are practical, and 'twas ever thus. Men may philosophize about how life began and where we are heading; women are concerned about feeding the kids today. No woman would ever, as Karl Marx did, spend years reading political philosophy in the British Museum while her child starved to death. Women don't take naturally to a search for the intangible and the abstract. The Positive Woman knows who she is and where she is going, and she will reach her goal because the longest journey starts with a very practical first step.

Amaury de Riencourt, in his book *Sex and Power in History*, shows that a successful society depends on a delicate balancing of different male and female factors. . . .

De Riencourt examines the fundamental, inherent differences between men and women. He argues that man is the more aggressive, rational, mentally creative, analytical-minded sex because of his early biological role as hunter and provider. Woman, on the other hand, represents stability, flexibility, reliance on intuition, and harmony with nature, stemming from her procreative function.

Where man is discursive, logical, abstract, or philosophical, woman tends to be emotional, personal, practical, or mystical. Each set of qualities is vital and complements the other. . . .

An effort to eliminate the differences by social engineering or legislative or constitutional tinkering cannot succeed, which is fortunate, but social relationships and spiritual values can be ruptured in the attempt. Thus the role reversals being forced upon high school students, under which guidance counselors urge reluctant girls to take "shop" and boys to take "home economics," further confuse a generation already unsure about its identity. They are as wrong as efforts to make a left-handed child right-handed.

"To be born female in this culture means. . .that there is something intrinsically wrong with you that you can never change, that your birthright is one of innate inferiority."

Women Are Oppressed By Men

Anne Wilson Schaef

Anne Wilson Schaef is a psychotherapist and a consultant in feminist therapy. Her years of working with many kinds of clients convinced her that there is something about our culture that contributes to the low feelings of self worth held by so many people she came into contact with, especially women. Ms. Schaef's analysis concludes that the cause is a pervading view of reality that dominates our culture and that excludes and belittles other views. She calls the dominant view the White Male System. In the viewpoint below, she explains this system and its effects on women.

As you read, consider the following questions:
1. According to Ms. Schaef, what is "the White Male System?" What are its four myths? What is the final, summarizing myth?
2. Why, according to Ms. Schaef, do women feel inferior. What is the "Original Sin concept"?
3. What are some of the ways women cope with the White Male System?
4. Is there any hope for change?

Let me explain what I mean by the White Male System....

We all live in it, but it is not reality. It is not the way the world is. Unfortunately, some of us do not recognize that it is a system and think it *is* reality or the way the world is.

The White Male System—and it is important to keep in mind that I am referring to a *system* here and not pointing a finger at specific individuals within it—controls almost every aspect of our culture. It makes our laws, runs our economy, sets our salaries, and decides when and if we will go to war or remain at home. It decides what *is* knowledge and how it is to be taught. Like any other system, it has both positive and negative qualities. But because it is only a system, it can be clarified, examined, and changed, both from within and without.

There are other systems within our culture. The Black System, the Chicano System, the Asian-American System, and the Native American System are completely enveloped in and frequently over-shadowed by the White Male System. As, of course, is the Female System, which includes women from the other ethnic systems as well as white women...

The Four Great Myths of the White Male System

The White Male System has four myths that feed it, sustain it, and (theoretically at least) justify it. These myths have been around for so long that most men are not even conscious of them. Many would deny their existence. Yet to challenge or doubt them is akin to heresy: they are sacred givens.

The first myth is that *the White Male System is the only thing that exists*. Because of this, the beliefs and perceptions of other systems— especially the Female System—are seen as sick, bad, crazy, stupid, ugly, and incompetent.

This myth is damaging in two ways. It limits women who want to explore their own perceptions and abilities, and it limits men who want to experience and learn from them.

Almost every woman has heard these words more than once: "You just don't know how the world is!" implying that the White Male System's view of the world is somehow "right." Women are also told time and again that they do not understand "reality." The White Male System is not reality. It is *a* reality, but it is not *the* reality, and women may very well have a reality all their own....

The second myth is that *the White Male System is innately superior*. Note that the first and second myths do not follow logically. If the White Male System is the only thing that exists, then how can it be superior and to what? Unfortunately, this inconsistency is of no concern to the White Male System.

At some level, the White Male System has recognized in spite of itself that other realities exist. It has gone on to define itself as superior to them while simultaneously believing that it is the only reality. Anyone who does not belong to this system is by definition innately inferior—and this includes members of all other racial groups, women, and the few white men who do not fit into the White Male System. . . .

From Nicole Hollander, *I'm in Training to Be Tall and Blonde.* Copyright © 1979 by Nicole Hollander. Reprinted with permission of St. Martin's Press.

The third myth is that *the White Male System knows and understands everything.* This is one reason why women so frequently look to men for advice and direction. Both sexes genuinely believe that men should and do know it all. In contrast to the first two myths, which are diametrically opposed, this myth follows the second one very nicely. If one is innately superior, then by rights one should be omniscient as well.

This myth is directly related to racial and sex-role stereotyping. A stereotype is no more than a definition of one group of persons by another who wishes to control it. Taken together, stereotypes support the myths of the White Male System.

No one would deny the fact that there are other people in our culture besides white men. Blacks, Chicanos, Native Americans, Asian Americans, and women are not exactly invisible. Precisely because they are different from white men, the White Male System must come to terms with them in some way. So it develops stereotypes that neatly describe and categorize these other groups. As long as the members of these groups go along with the stereotypes, they support the illusion that the White Male System knows and understands everything. If white men say that women are weak, and women behave as if they are weak, then who can argue with the myth?...

The fourth and final myth of the White Male System is that *it is possible to be totally logical, rational, and objective.* The problem with this myth is that one must constantly do battle with the ways in which one is not all of these things. One must continually overcome and deny any tendencies toward illogical, irrational, subjective, or intuitive thoughts or behaviors.

Members of the White Male System spend a lot of time and energy telling women that females are by nature not logical, rational, or objective. Often they do so in highly emotional ways!...

Living according to these myths can mean living in ignorance. For example, the only way to maintain the myth of knowing and understanding everything is to *ignore* a whole universe of other information. When one clings to the myth of innate superiority, one must constantly overlook the virtues and abilities of others....

All four myths of the White Male System can be summarized by another that is almost always unspoken but nevertheless present and real. This final myth is that *it is possible for one to be God.* If the White Male System is the only system that exists, if white males are innately superior, if they know and understand everything, and if they can be totally logical, rational and objective, then they can be God—at least, the way the White Male System defines God....

The Original Sin of Being Born Female

Since the women's movement has become more accepted and acceptable, dislike and distrust of other women has become more subtle, but it is still there....

In general, women feel relatively safe attacking other women. We are not dependent on each other for our identity, so what does it matter? This ongoing antipathy has severely hindered the growth and maturation of the Female System. The White Male System has used its observation of women inflicting pain on one another to discount the Female System.

When women say, "I do not like or trust other women," what we are really saying is, "I don't like myself." And this in turn can be expanded to "I don't like femaleness."....

To be born female in this culture means that you are born "tainted," that there is something intrinsically wrong with you that you can never change, that your birthright is one of innate inferiority. I am not implying that this must remain so. I do believe that we must know this and understand it as a given before it can be worked through and put to rest.

Regardless of how confident or competent a woman is, she struggles with this "given" in life....

According to the theological concept of original sin, there is no real justification by works. Women can never absolve themselves of their Original Sin of Being Born Female. There is no "right thing" we can do to atone for it even though we spend much of our time and creative energy trying to....

Saluting the Patriarchy

Women are equal to men in susceptibility to patriarchal attitudes; that is why women did not (as some expected) change the world when they got the vote. Instead we became capably functioning members of the patriarchy: saluted its flag, joined its armies, voted for its candidates and continued to send the children we bore and raised to go and conquer and, incidentally, die. If we attempt to speak of revolution, of the drastic in-depth change necessary to reverse the course of our world, we must speak of identifying and pulling out the patriarch in each of us; similarly we must speak of ending our submission, shifting our minds, making conscious choices and being victims no longer. We must do this within the context of the movement for social change, not simply as an analysis of "what's wrong out there." In this case as in most others, the enemy turns out to be not just "them," but us, too.

Shelley Douglass, "Patriarchy: A Definition," *IFOR Report* (International Fellowship of Reconciliation), December 1982.

Many women feel that they cannot be whole without a man. We look to men to provide us with wholeness. When this fails, we blame ourselves and feel even worse. Some women prefer the status of being divorced to that of being single. To them, having had a man at one time is better than never having had one.

Women are often terrified of being alone. Being "connected" to someone else—a man—ensures their survival. They do not understand that even when no one else is around they are still with someone—themselves.

Remember that in the Original Sin concept, we can only be "saved" with the help and intervention of an outside intermediary. We are taught that we will be all right if we can only attach ourselves to an innately superior being, a man, who will then intercede for us. We will feel good again. We will be absolved of being born female. What this means, of course, is that we see other women as competitors for the "goodies"—male validation and approval. Men also participate in this thinking by setting up a situation that suggests "You and her fight—over me and for my attention." . . .

Many women work hard to do all the "right" things. They find nice men, attach themselves, produce lovely children (male children are especially important), devote themselves to homemaking, and still feel unhappy. Then they assume that they are at fault. "I have done everything this culture has told me to do," their unconscious tells them, "but still I have not been absolved of my Original Sin of Being Born Female. There must be something wrong with me!" Few question the culture that tells women they will feel better if and only if they are saved by male validation and approval. . . .

Because our position in this culture is so shaky, we have learned to lie. We lie to men and to other women, but mostly we lie to ourselves. We lie about who we are and about what we want and need. By learning to lie, we feel that we can carve out a niche for ourselves, but what this really does is to intensify our isolation and sense of not belonging. Once we start being honest with ourselves and with other women, though, our feelings of isolation lessen.

Being Like Men

Women frequently go along with the expectations of the White Male System in order to win acceptance. Most of us do this in one of two ways: we either try to act out the White Male System's definition of the traditional "proper" woman, or we try to be "like men." . . .

Many women believe that the only road to success is to act like men and beat them at their own game. Some women embrace the tenets of the White Male System more avidly than men themselves do. This tactic can be self-defeating, however. If women are too successful, they are punished. We try to be intelligent—but our intelligence must never threaten men. We try to be competent—but our competence must never overshadow that of men. . . .

Women who buy into the White Male System often use power—when they get it—like men: against other women and to destroy them. Our dislike and distrust of femaleness goes very deep. . . .

Because it refuses to see the worth and meaning inherent in differences and perceives them as threats to be overcome, the White Male System is a closed system. It stifles creativity and devours itself from within. It wastes and loses energy and is moving toward a state of entropy. . . .

It is important for women *and* men to see that the White Male System is just that—a system. It is not reality. It is not the way the world is. Reality is difficult if not impossible to change, but a system can be changed, even if it means a struggle. That gives us hope. If we can learn to recognize that there is at least one other system besides the

White Male System, we can begin to see the value of still other systems and realities. We can begin to pay closer attention to the Black, Chicano, Asian-American, and Native American systems and learn from them as well. It is only then that we will begin to grow to our fullest capacity as human beings.

"The older the girl grows, the more highly conditioned she becomes in the art of exploiting others."

Women Are the Oppressors of Men

Esther Vilar

Born in Argentina in 1931 to German parents, Esther Vilar is trained as a physician. Besides working as a staff doctor in a Bavarian hospital, she has held many different kinds of jobs including translator, saleswoman, assembly-line worker, and shoe model. In the following viewpoint, she expresses her belief that women, far from being oppressed, are in fact the oppressors of unwitting men.

As you read, consider the following questions:
1. According to Ms. Vilar, why do women not make use of what intellectual capabilities they might have?
2. What does she believe women want out of life?
3. What methods does Ms. Vilar say women use to make men do what women want them to?
4. What do you think of her views of men and women and their relationships?

Women let men work for them, think for them, and take on their responsibilities—in fact, they exploit them. Yet, since men are strong, intelligent, and imaginative, while women are weak, unimaginative, and stupid, why isn't it men who exploit women?

Could it be that strength, intelligence, and imagination are not prerequisites for power but merely qualifications for slavery? Could it be that the world is not being ruled by experts but by beings who are not fit for anything else—by women? And if this is so, how do women manage it so that their victims do not feel themselves cheated and humiliated, but rather believe themselves to be what they are least of all—masters of the universe? How do women manage to instill in men this sense of pride and superiority that inspires them to ever greater achievements?...

Training with Praise

One of the most useful factors in the conditioning of a man is *praise*. Its effect is better and much more lasting than say, sex, as it may be continued throughout a man's life. Furthermore, if praise is applied in the correct dosage, a woman will never need to scold. Any man who is accustomed to a conditional dosage of praise will interpret its absence as displeasure.

Training by means of praise has the following advantages: it makes the object of praise dependent (for praise to be worth something, it has to come from a higher source, thus the object of praise lifts the praise-giver to a superior level); it creates an addict (without praise, he soon no longer knows whether or not he is worth something and forgets the ability to identify with himself); it increases his productivity (praise is most effectively meted out not for the same achievements, but for increasingly higher ones).

The moment a male child has been rewarded by a warm smile and by the customary inane kind of encouraging adult baby talk for using his pot and not wetting his bed, or for drinking the last drop in his bottle, he is caught up in a vicious circle. He will repeat the actions which called forth praise and endearments and, if at any time recognition is not granted, he will do everything in his power to regain it. The happiness he feels when praise is restored will already have assumed the proportions of an addiction.

During the first two years of life, a mother does not discriminate between boys and girls. The female infant is submitted to the same form of manipulation until the principles of hygiene are absorbed, but from that moment on, the education of the two sexes follows very different paths. The older the girl grows, the more highly conditioned she becomes in the art of exploiting others, while a boy is increasingly manipulated into becoming an object of exploitation....

Long before man is in a position to choose his own way of life, he will have formed the necessary addiction to praise. He will be happy only when his work brings him praise and, because he is an addict, his need will increase—and with it the type of achievement so much praised by his woman. This male need could, of course, be satisfied by another man, but, as each man is working feverishly in the interest of his own addiction, he has no time to help others. Indeed man exists, as it were, in a state of constant antagonistic competition with other men. It is one of the reasons why he loses no time in getting his own private panegyrist, one whose praise will be his exclusive right, someone who will always be at home waiting to tell him when he has been good and just how good he has been. It is apparently only by chance that woman is best suited to this role: but in fact, she has been preparing all her life for it, waiting to assume it. . . .

"Well, I guess the honeymoon is over.
She's complaining about the way I do the laundry."

Bill Hoest, *Parade* Magazine. Reprinted with permission.

To avoid having to exert effort, all a woman has to do is heave a sigh and indicate that she, "as a woman," is simply not capable of the task. If she merely hints to a man, preferably with witnesses present, that he drives so much better than she does, she has found herself a chauffeur for life. Look at the highways—they are full of women being driven by their husband-chauffeurs. A woman will say that she cannot possibly, "as a woman," go to a cafe or a theater or a restaurant by herself. . . .

Love

Man has been manipulated by woman to the point where he cannot live without her and therefore will do anything she asks of him. He fights for his life and calls it *love*. There are even men who will threaten their idolized female with suicide unless she accepts him. Not that this is much of a risk for them—they have nothing to lose.

Woman, nevertheless, is incapable of living without man. Like a queen bee, she cannot survive on her own. She, too, is fighting for her life, and she, too, calls it *love*. They each need one another, in fact, and it seems therefore that they share at least *one* sentiment. The cause, nature, and consequences of this sentiment, however, differ as much as do the sexes.

Money, Status, Power

"Nothing has changed. I grew up with women's lib but nothing has changed. No matter what they tell you, women still want the same things they've always wanted in a man. Money. Status. Power."

Anonymous man quoted by Anthony Brandt in "Feminism: A Man's View," *Harper's Bazaar*, August 1983.

To a woman love means power, to a man enslavement. Love provides woman with an excuse for financial exploitation, man with an emotionally charged excuse. "For the sake of love" woman will do things that are of advantage only to herself, while man does only those things that will harm him. When a woman marries, she gives up her career "for the sake of love." When a man marries, he will have to work for two "for the sake of love." For both sexes, love is a fight for survival. But the one survives only by being victorious, the other only by being defeated. It is a paradox that women can also make their greatest gains during moments of utter passivity and that the word "love" endows them with a halo of selflessness, even at the moment of their most pitiless deception of man.

As a result of "love," man is able to hide his cowardly self-deception behind a smoke screen of sentiment. He is able to make himself believe that his senseless enslavement to woman and her hostages is more than an act of honor, it has a higher purpose. He is entirely happy in his role as a slave and has arrived at the goal he has so long desired. Since woman gains nothing but one advantage after another from the situation as it stands today, things will never change. The system forces her to be corrupt, but no one is going to worry about that. Since one can expect nothing from a woman but *love*, it will remain the currency for any need she might have. Man, her slave, will continue to use his energies only according to his conditioning and never to his own advantage. He will achieve greater goals, and the more he achieves, the farther women will become alienated from him. The more he tries to ingratiate himself with her, the more demanding she will become; the more he desires her, the less she will find him desirable; the more comforts he provides for her, the more indolent, stupid, and inhuman she will become—and man will grow lonelier as a result.

Pitiless Women

Only woman can break the vicious circle of man's manipulation and exploitation—but she will not do it. There is absolutely no compelling reason why she should. It is useless to appeal to her feelings, for she is callous and knows no pity. And so the world will go on, sinking deeper and deeper into this morass of kitsch, barbarism, and inanity called *femininity*. And man, that wonderful dreamer, will never awaken from his dream.

"Because of job segregation and pay inequity, a woman head of household today is six times as likely as a man in her position to be poor."

Women Are Economically Oppressed

Clarice Stasz

Clarice Stasz, a professor of sociology at Sonoma State University, has written a book called *The American Nightmare: The Success Ideal and Work Discrimination.* Its subject matter includes some of the issues that are discussed in the viewpoint below. Here she describes the inequities faced by the woman worker in America.

As you read, consider the following questions:
1. According to Ms. Stasz, why are more women working today than a few years ago?
2. What does she believe are some of the real reasons that women don't earn as much money as men?
3. What is the "comparable pay" concept? What are some of the problems and advantages Ms. Stasz sees with this concept?

Clarice Stasz, "Room at the Bottom," *Working Papers,* January/February 1982.

Many Americans today are worrying more about "reverse discrimination" than about the...downgrading of affirmative action.

How much justice do women in fact experience?...

Let's begin with the most obvious trend—the increase in the number and proportion of women in the labor market, which now stands at about 40 percent of all full-time employees. In the 1960s this increased participation was linked to changes in family planning (the number and spacing of children), the increased educational level of women, and the mushrooming of clerical positions available.

In the 1970s two new reasons for women's participation emerged. First, with the development of the stagflation economy, fewer families could meet basic needs with only one salary, forcing women to share the breadwinning.

The second, ironically enough, is that more women are working because of the break-up of family ties. Between 1968 and 1978 the number of women heads of families increased by 54 percent to 8.2 million. Consequently, one out of every five female employees is separated, divorced, or widowed. When one adds in the 11 million single women, half of all wage-earning women are the sole support of themselves and others. Yet they face a labor market based on the outmoded assumption that women are marginal or temporary workers, that they only want pin money, or that they will quit when they marry or have a first child. In reality, of course, women—like men—work to survive.

Gap in Earnings

The current gap between men's and women's earnings is a clear indication that the labor market ignores this. Counting only full-time employees, men take home about $1.75 for every dollar earned by women. And this gap is widening: in 1977 men earned $1.69 for every dollar earned by women. In fact, as women heads of households enter the labor market the statistics get worse. In 1959 a white female with responsibility for a family earned 75 cents to every dollar earned by a white male family head; today she earns 59 cents. (Half of women heading households make less than $190 a week before payroll deductions.)

The bottom line is startling: even allowing for discrepancies in education, experience, age, regional variation, and occupational prestige, Department of Labor statistics (1975 data) calculate that a white woman earns about half of a white man's salary. For black and Mexican-American women the proportion is even lower...

Hand in hand with the pay gap is the unemployment gap. As over the past three decades, women are currently 50 percent more likely to be unemployed than men are. The actual rate may be even higher, since women are more prone to accept part-time or seasonal work when they actually need a full-time job, and there are an increasing number of high turnover jobs available to women...

66

One reason often advanced for the poor opportunities available to women is that they are not equivalent workers with men—that they lack education, experience, loyalty, and so forth. Some economists contend that women's "human capital" isn't well developed...

Given that the bulk of jobs require on-the-job training, we must look elsewhere for an explanation of women's position in the labor market.

"Women's Work"

One problem that women continue to face is the stubborn persistence of cultural stereotype. If there are few women distilling whiskey, vulcanizing rubber, or piloting helicopters, it is partly because counselors, school admissions committees, union officials, and personnel executives still have trouble imagining such a thing. Gatekeepers to jobs identify women as sales clerks, secretaries, nurses, clothing makers, and waitresses; women who are looking for a job rather than a fight must accept the identity.

YOU BOTH ARE MY TWO BEST EMPLOYEES..

SO BILL.. IM PROMOTING YOU TO PRESIDENT..

AND JANE.. I WANT YOU TO TAKE OVER MY PLANT...

Mike Peters, *Dayton Daily News*. Reprinted with permission.

Unfortunately, this often leaves them ghettoized in a low wage workforce. Clerical work, for example, is women's work, whose wages are set low and peak quickly...

The circular logic of ghettoization then takes over. Since the jobs that women do are low paid, by definition "women's jobs" become inferior jobs. A striking reflection of this can be seen in the Department of Labor's *Dictionary of Occupational Titles,* where all the jobs assigned to women are systematically underevaluated. Thus foster

mother, child care attendant, practical nurse, and nursery school attendant rank among the lowest jobs possible, slightly below horse pusher
and well below marine mammal handler . . .

As customs change, and men take up working with children, the
value assigned to those jobs increases. In recent years the salary scale
in elementary school teaching, for example, has increased at a much
faster than average rate. The opposite is also true—as more women
embark on careers in accounting, the pay in some areas of the profession is stagnating.

Moreover, in female-dominated professions like library work or
social services, men advance more rapidly into the better paid administrative positions. The proportion of school principals and heads
of social work departments who are men is far higher than the male
proportion of all school teachers and social workers . . .

The cumulative effect of these figures typically means that at the
end of twenty-five years a man worker will have earned $76,000 more
than a woman worker. Promotion and pay inequities have compound
effects as the years go by and the pay gap multiplies.

Legislated Solutions

In the course of the last two decades, these inequities have been
addressed by all three branches of the government, and the number
and variety of federal laws and regulations that apply to equal opportunity suggest a comprehensive policy . . .

Seemingly, this body of laws and regulations should provide equal
opportunity for women workers. Affirmative Action should mean that
along with goods and services, federal contracts also buy increased
equality for American workers . . .

This has, of course, not been the result of these policies. The sex-
defined dual labor market seems impervious to them. One explanation is that the labor market discriminates both within a given
workplace *and* by industry or professional job category. While an
employer who assigns an unskilled woman is clearly in violation, the
laws and regulations do not apply to workplaces where all the jobs
are poorly paid. In small, low profit firms where employment is often
seasonal or part-time, there is no internal discrimination because
everyone is paid poorly. But law does not address the issue of why
all the workers in such firms are women.

In the same way, the civil rights laws do not reach areas where
women are customarily segregated by occupation. In 1978 a group
of nurses in Denver sued the city for paying them less than tree trimmers, sign painters, and tire servicers. They lost the case because the
employer (in this case the city) is not required to change the wage
structure of its jobs, but only refrain from assigning men and women
to those jobs discriminatorily. The judge ruled that the employer is
not liable for the fact that (low paid) nurses are women and (better
paid) tree trimmers are men. The judicial system was unwilling to
rule against an *economic system* that has assigned women to lower pay-

ing jobs...

Thus, the women who do manage to make their way out of dead-end jobs have almost invariably done so by coat-tailing on men's professions. The current structure of the labor market dictates that the best opportunities will be in a large metropolitan firm that is at least 85 percent male and heavily capital intensive. The average woman will not find equity with men in such a firm, but she will be likely to receive a higher salary on the woman's scale...

The failure of civil rights legislation to reach the structural ghettoization of the typing pool is at least partly caused by its implicit belief that women should be shifted into men's jobs, but men need not be considered for women's. For sex-typing in the labor market to really change, the very idea of "women's work" must be challenged. Because affirmative action laws are primarily directed at integrating the largely white male elite, they have not reached the problem of small, heavily female, secondary labor market firms...

Working Women

	% of Women in Major Occupation Groups	Women's Share of Major Occupation Groups
Clerical workers	34.7%	80.5%
Service workers	17.1	59.2
Professional & technical workers	17.0	44.6
Operatives (except transport)	9.7	19.8
Managers & administrators	7.4	27.5
Sales workers	6.8	45.4
Craft & kindred workers	1.9	6.3
Transport equipment operatives	0.7	8.9
Laborers	1.2	11.5
Private household workers	2.3	96.5
Farm workers	1.1	17.8

Department of Labor statistics.

The rules, geared unrealistically to upward mobility, say only that the doors to elite jobs must be opened to those once excluded. So long as only women enter whole categories of jobs or entry level slots, structural inequities will be difficult to fight...

Comparable Pay

What policy, therefore, would address these structural issues of equal opportunity? One concept that is sometimes brought up in connection with affirmative action suits is that of comparable pay. Comparable pay policies would require equal pay scales for jobs that re-quire equivalent, rather than identical, skills, responsibility, and effort.

Once men were held to be the sole support of families and their positions automatically received higher salaries and status. As "scientific management" techniques evolved, personnel directors attempted to evaluate jobs—and assign salaries—by a point system. A recent EEOC review of their evaluation instruments discovered they had little to do with job difficulty or skill, and often had little relevance to the

America's Workers

	Women	Men	Women's Income as % of Men's
Americans Age 15 & older (1980)	91,400,000	83,800,000	
Employed Americans	44,000,000	58,000,000	
Unemployment rate 1981	6.8%	6.3%	
Median Income			
8th grade Education or less	$ 9000	$15,000	63 %
High school education	12,000	20,500	59.9
Some college	14,300	22,500	63.6
College graduate	17,800	28,000	63.2
Weekly Median Earnings in Selected Occupations			
Accountant	$473	$601	78%
Carpenter	350	401	87
Clerical worker	220	328	67
Computer specialists	355	488	73
Engineers	371	547	68
Nurses	326	344	95
Sales workers	190	366	52
Secretary	304	285	107
All occupations 1980	$215	$357	60.2%

Department of Labor statistics.

jobs they attempted to evaluate.

Today job evaluation formulas give high points to lifting heavy objects, obvious physical danger, supervisory responsibilities, and the tending of goods and property. They undervalue frequent lifting of light objects, environmental stress, interpersonal skills, and direct services to people. Put simply, men's work is still considered to be more valuable than women's.

Washington State's government parking lot employees, who need only have a driver's licnese, earn almost as much as entry-level secretaries, who must be able to type fifty words a minute with no more than one error, take shorthand and dictaphone transcription, oversee an office of clerks, run business machines, and understand numerous office practices. A consulting firm's recent estimate of the two jobs concluded that the secretaries were worth about $400 a month more than they were getting. . .

The implementation of genuine comparable pay could have radical consequences. It would mean that jobs unattractive to men because of low salaries, in particular clerical work, would become more appealing to them. Then, as men entered new job categories, the circular logic that undervalued those jobs would be thrown in reverse. "Women's work" would begin to lose its subservient, marginal connotation, and its position in the economy would be assigned a more realistic value.

Though rich in promise, however, comparable pay will not resolve all the inequities in the labor market. . .

Nevertheless, comparable pay begins to address the assumptions by which places in that market are allocated. . .

Cuts in welfare, CETA, Social Security, and other human service programs exacerbate the feminization of poverty. Because of job segregation and pay inequity, a woman head of household today is six times as likely as a man in her position to be poor. Women's poverty is likely to persist, because her work does not accrue rewards with experience. The National Advisory Council on Economic Opportunity projects that if current trends continue, 100 percent of "poor" families will be headed by women by the year 2000. Any women's agenda for the 1980s will have to be based on this fundamental understanding of the status of women's work. Otherwise we will not be able to go beyond gender tokenism.

"The earnings gap is due to the fact that women do not do the same work as men, and they get different pay for different work."

Women Are Not Economically Oppressed

Judith Finn

A former researcher and teacher of political science, Judith Finn describes herself as a homemaker. In April of 1981, she testified before the U.S. Senate Committee on Labor and Human Resources. Her testimony, the viewpoint below, defends the lower pay women receive. In it she states several reasons for the seeming inequity which she believes is justified.

As you read, consider the following questions:
1. According to Mrs. Finn, how much of the pay inequity between men and women is due to unfair discrimination against women?
2. According to Mrs. Finn, women hold different jobs than men do because of different "job attributes." What are some of these differences?
3. What concerns Mrs. Finn more than the possibilites of discrimination?

Judith Finn, Testimony to the U.S. Senate Committee on Labor and Human Resources, April 21, 1981.

I am Judith Finn. I am a homemaker from Oak Ridge, Tennessee. I was trained as an economist and political scientist, and I worked for several years doing public policy research and teaching political science.

Women in the labor force earn about 63 percent as much as men. This has been cited by witnesses before this committee as evidence of widespread sex discrimination in employment. However, studies by economists on the nature of this earnings gap have found no hard evidence at all that any significant portion of this gap is due to sex discrimination.

The earnings gap is due to the fact that women do not do the same work as men, and they get different pay for different work. When women are doing the same job as men, the fact is they do receive equal pay for equal work. The authors of a survey of the economic literature on this subject sponsored by the Committee on the Status of Women in the Economics Profession and published by the American Economics Association concluded that "... perhaps the sole consistent result of the empirical studies surveyed is that sex discrimination in the form of unequal pay for equal work is of little, if any, quantitative significance."

Of course, to conclude that unequal pay for equal work is not "of any quantitative significance" is not to deny that violations of the Equal Pay act occur, merely that such violations can explain only a negligible portion of the earnings gap. There are two reasons for this.

First, if we define "equal work" methodologically by controlling for differences in education, experience, detailed differences in occupation, and job level, etc., then we can explain virtually all of the earnings gap. Just as important is that men and women tend to hold different kinds of jobs, and the kinds held by women tend to be lower-paying jobs. Since men and women are not doing the same work very much of the time, unequal pay for doing the same work could not explain much of the earnings gap even if the studies did find significant pay inequalities for the same work.

Different Pay for Different Work

Since pay differences are almost completely caused by differences in jobs rather than the failure to obtain equal pay for equal work, understanding the earnings gap requires an explanation of the reasons why women, on the average, hold lower-paying jobs than men. Women have different job-related attributes and different amounts of these attributes than men.

These differences, which are due to the dual role that the majority of women in this country still choose to play, explain most, if not all, of the earnings gap. I will briefly summarize these differences.

1. *Women have different educational attributes.* Women receive as much education as men today, but women compare unfavorably with men in the kind of education they receive. Women tend to predominate in fields of study where salaries are depressed by ex-

cess supply, like humanities, social science, and education, while men study in fields where salaries are high, like engineering, computer science, and accounting.

Dramatic changes are occurring in this regard. For example, the proportion of women enrolling in the high-paying fields of engineering, business, and medicine has increased several fold in the past decade. But we cannot expect these changes to signal equality of educational attainment in the near future because women still record mathematical aptitude well below that of men, and this limits their likelihood of success in many of the predominantly male fields.

2. *Women invest less in on-the-job training.* Women's investment in on-the-job training comes to only a fraction of the amount invested by men. From a narrow economic point of view this is rational behavior on the part of women who expect to restrict their work effort in order to raise a family. However, on-the-job training is an important factor influencing earnings. Women's lower level of training has been shown to be an important factor in the earnings gap between men and women.

Marriage Affects Earning Power

With women the key variable is marriage. Even before "affirmative action" quotas, women in their 30s who had worked continuously since high school earned slightly *more* than men in their 30s who had worked continuously since high school. Female academics earned slightly *more* than male academics when neither were married—again even before "affirmative action"—and unmarried female PhDs became full professors to a slightly *greater* extent than did unmarried male PhDs. In short, the male-female differences in incomes and occupations are largely differences between married women and all other persons.

Thomas Sowell, *Knowledge and Decisions,*, Basic Books, 1980.

---

3. *Women have less work experience.* On average, women have fewer years of work experience than men. This is partly due to higher unemployment, but more importantly to the fact that women drop out of the labor force to pursue family responsibilities associated with child bearing and child rearing.

4. *Women work fewer hours.* Women work part-time far more often than men. But more importantly women who work full-time (more than 35 hours per week) also work shorter hours, 10 percent fewer hours than men who work full-time. In addition, women have nearly 50 percent higher absences from work than men.

5. *Women have shorter job tenure.* Job tenure, defined as the length of time an employee has worked steadily for the same employer, has been shown to be an important factor affecting salaries. On average, persons having more tenure with their current employer report higher

salaries than others who are similar in other respects, even others who have the same total number of years of work experience. Thus it is significant that men report nearly twice as much job tenure as women: the median is 4.5 years for men and 2.6 years for women. The greater job tenure of men is attributed to two factors depressing the average for women. A relatively large proportion of women workers are under age 25 where job tenure is at a minimum. Also many women leave the work force at least once during their working lives because of family responsibilities.

6. *Women have less geographic mobility.* Compared with men, women are less willing to move to another location to get a job when unemployed or to get a better job when employed. Single women, like men, experience increased earnings when they move, but married women do not. On the average, their family income goes up as a result of the move, but the wife is frequently following her husband in these cases, and on average, receives lower earnings as a result of temporary unemployment.

Lower Motivation

7. *Women are less motivated to maximize earnings and have different work-related values.* There are few good measures of male/female differences in motivation which is unquestionably an important determinant of salary differences. We do know that among college students, males place a higher value on achieving financial success than their female counterparts. Case studies of differences in motivation between male and female employees in the same firm have also indicated sex differences in motivation which are directly related to promotion up the ladder. There is evidence that women value non-salary characteristics in their jobs, like pleasant inter-personal relationships, pleasant working conditions, and a good location more than men. This implies that, on the average, women trade-off salary for these other working conditions more frequently than men.

It is entirely plausible that these differences in job-related attributes explain the entire earnings gap. However, neither the data nor the methods that have been brought to bear on this issue are adequate to show conclusively that male/female differences in characteristics and behavior are (or are not) sufficient to explain the differences in average salaries. We can be sure that these differences explain most, if not all, of the earnings gap. The problem is that we have no direct measurement of discrimination.

The method used by economists is to explain the difference in earnings using a mathematical model, as well as possible with the data available, and then to attribute the unexplained residual to sex discrimination. But in fact the existence of a residual does not prove that discrimination has occurred. The residual also includes the effects of unmeasured and improperly measured differences in male/female productivity. Not all economists working in this area mistakenly assert that the residual is a measure of sex discrimination, but the important point here is that those who do claim to have found discrimination have only the existence of the residual upon which to base this claim.

Congressional Responsibility

While it is true that the evidence is inconclusive, it is equally true that the differences in the choices that women make explain most, if not all, of the earnings gap. Therefore, what is the proper role for Congress here? Surely, it is not the role of Congress to narrow the wage gap by forcing or encouraging women to change their labor market behavior and increase their human capital and become more like men. We support the efforts of the Equal Employment Opportunity Commission to combat sex discrimination. However, this should not be construed to mean that we are asking for more government regulations, more quotas, and more special programs for women. A good case can be made that the interests of women as well as the economy would be better served by a reform of the adverse effect of existing regulations. In his review of antibias programs Professor Richard Lester of Princeton concluded that "the application of antibias programs . . . has involved disregard of individual differences, has challenged merit as the basis for promotion and pay, and has shown a lack of concern for the efficient use of resources."

It is the responsibility of Congress to see that the cures for problems of discrimination in employment are not worse than the problems themselves. We cannot be sure that sex discrimination is an important determinant of women's earnings, and except for isolated case studies, it has never been documented to exist. We are, however, increasingly sure that government regulation of the economy is hurting productivity. Because women depend on a healthy growing economy even more than men, the negative impact of antidiscrimination regulations are just as important to women as sex discrimination itself. We urge this committee to seriously consider this issue as it evaluates demands for further regulation.

Distinguishing Between Fact and Opinion

This activity is designed to help develop the basic reading and thinking skill of distinguishing between fact and opinion. Consider the following statement as an example. "Only women are able to bear children." This statement is a fact which no one would deny. But consider a statement like this: "Women who don't recognize the fact that they can be fulfilled as human beings only by carrying out their biological function of being mothers are causing broken families and social unrest." Such a statement is clearly an expressed opinion. Both the idea of woman's fulfillment coming only through motherhood *and* the suggestion that not concurring with that belief causes society's social and family unrest would be loudly challenged by many people.

When investigating controversial issues it is important that one be able to distinguish between statements of fact and statements of opinion.

The following statements are taken from the viewpoints in this chapter. Consider each statement carefully. *Mark O for any statement you feel is an opinion or interpretation of facts. Mark F for any statement you believe is a fact.*

If you are doing this activity as the member of a class or group, compare your answers with those of other class or group members. Be able to defend your answers. You may discover that others will come to different conclusions than you. Listening to the reasons others present for their answers may give you valuable insights in distinguishing between fact and opinion.

If you are reading this book alone, ask others if they agree with your answers. You too will find this interaction very valuable.

O = opinion
F = fact

1. Women can save more money by their managerial talents inside the home than they can bring into it by outside work.
2. Great men have great mothers.
3. Love and children and home are good, but they are not the whole world.
4. Our culture does not permit women to accept or gratify their basic need to grow and fulfill their potentialities as human beings, a need which is not solely defined by their sexual role.
5. There are countless physical differences between men and women.
6. The overriding psychological need of a woman is to love something alive.
7. Men are philosophers, women are practical, and 'twas ever thus.
8. No woman would ever, as Karl Marx did, spend years reading political philosophy in the British museum while her child starved to death.
9. Where man is discursive, logical, abstract, or philosophical, woman tends to be emotional, personal, practical, or mystical.
10. Both sexes genuinely believe that men should and do know it all.
11. To be born female in this culture means that you are born "tainted," that there is something intrinsically wrong with you that you can never change, that your birthright is one of innate inferiority.
12. Many women feel they cannot be whole without a man.
13. Woman is incapable of living without man.
14. To a woman love means power, to a man enslavement.
15. In the 1970s with the development of the stagflation economy, fewer families could meet basic needs with only one salary, forcing women to share the breadwinning.
16. Counting only full-time employees, men take home about $1.75 for every dollar earned by women.
17. In female-dominated professions like library work or social services, men advance more rapidly into the better paid administrative positions.
18. The earnings gap is due to the fact that women do not do the same work as men, and they get different pay for different work.

Bibliography

The following list of periodical articles deals with the subject matter of this chapter.

Gina Allen	"How Your Daughter Grows Up to Be a Man," *The Humanist*, March/April 1980.
L.B. Andrews	"As the Twig is Bent," *Parents*, February 1983.
Sey Chessler	"I was Born with a Twin..." *Ms.*, July/August 1982.
Christianity & Crisis	Special issue: "Feminism: A Deeper Look," April 2, 1982.
Jay Cocks & Others	"How Long Till Equality?" *Time*, July 12, 1982.
Lorraine Davis, Editor	"Women Now: The Open Doors," *Vogue,* June 1983.
Midge Decter	"Who Speaks for Women?" *Newsweek*, April 15, 1980.
Nancy Doyle	"Women's Changing Place: A Look at Sexism," Public Affairs Pamphlet No. 509, 381 Park Avenue South, New York 10016, 1979.
Jo Durden-Smith & Diane DeSimone	"Is There a Superior Sex?" *Playboy*, May 1982.
Barbara Ehrenreich & Karin Stallard	"The Nouveau Poor," *Ms.*, July/August 1982.
Riane Eisler	"The Global Impact of Sexual Equality," *The Humanist*, May/June 1981.
Riane Eisler	"Women's Rights and Human Rights," *The Humanist,* November/December 1980.
Eleanor Flexner	"Women's Rights—Unfinished Business," Public Affairs Pamphlet No. 469, 381 Park Avenue South, New York 10016, 1979.
George Gilder	The Myths of Racial and Sexual Discrimination," *National Review*, November 14, 1980.
Carol Gilligan	"Why Should a Woman Be More Like a Man?" *Psychology Today*, June 1982.
Lloyd Gite	"How Have Women's Changing Roles Changed You?" *Essense*, November 1982.
Suzanne Gordon	"The Feminist Mystique," *Working Papers*, July/August 1981.
Patricia Albjerg Graham	"The Cult of True Womanhood," *Vital Speeches*, April 15, 1983.
Sheila Graham	"The Battle of the Sexes—It's Killing Us All," *The Plain Truth*, March 1982.

Marvin Harris

"Why It's Not the Same Old America," Section , II, *Psychology Today*, August 1981.

Barbara Grizzuti Harrison

Pro and Con: "What Do Women Want?" *Harper's*, October 1981.

Natalie Jaffe

"Men's Jobs for Women: Toward Occupational Equality," Public Affairs Pamphlet No. 606, 381 Park Avenue South, New York 10016, 1980.

Elizabeth Janeway

"Women:'We've Come a Short Way, Baby,'" *U.S. News & World Report*, October 6, 1980.

Michael Levin

"Feminism and Thought Control," *Commentary*, June 1982.

Dan Morris

"Now No One Does the Dishes," *U.S. Catholic*, June 1982.

Diana Pearce
& Hariette McAdoo

"Women and Children: Alone and in Poverty," Washington, D.C., National Advisory Council on Economic Opportunity, September 1981. Available from Diana Pearce, The Center for National Policy Review, Catholic University Law School, Washington, DC 20064.

Mary Pellaver

"Violence Against Women: The Theological Dimension," *Christianity & Crisis*, May 30, 1983.

The Progressive

"Women's Work," August 1, 1981.

Maria Riley

"What Do Women Want?" *America*, July 26, 1980.

Phyllis Schlafly

"Don't Let the Courts Draft Women," *The Phyllis Schlafly Report*, P.O. Box 618, Alton, IL 62002, January 1981.

Phyllis Schlafly

"The Unfairness of Unisex Insurance Laws," *The Phyllis Schlafly Report*, P.O. Box 618, Alton, IL 62002, May 1983.

Sue Shellenbarger

"As More Women Take Jobs, They Affect Ads, Politics, Family Life," *Wall Street Journal*, June 29, 1982.

U.S. Department of Labor

"The Female-Male Earnings Gap: A Review of Employment and Earnings Issues," Washington, D.C., Bureau of Labor Statistics, Report 673, September 1982.

Patsy Vigderman

"Two-Timing Women: The Supermom Myth," *Working Papers*, November/December 1981.

Richard A. Vigueril

"The Real 'Women's Issues,'" *Conservative Digest*, October 1982.

James M. Wall

"The Real Issue for Women Is Power," *The Christian Century*, October 27, 1982.

Naomi Weisstein

"Tired of Arguing about Biological Inferiority?" *Ms.*, November 1982.

Ellen Willis

"The Politics of Dependency," *Ms.*, July/August 1982.

Do Men
Need Liberating?

"The alleged discrimination against women in employment, abortion, and miscellaneous areas is insignificant compared to that against men in crime and punishment, employment, and domestic relations."

Men Need Liberating from Unfair Laws

Richard F. Doyle

Richard Doyle joined with several other men in 1972 to found the Men's Rights Association (M.R.A.). A national organization, the M.R.A. is concerned primarily with divorce reform but also with combatting what it sees as unfair social pressures from feminists and others who work to reduce male rights in an attempt to secure female rights. Mr. Doyle and his organization believe that it is men who are unfairly treated by society. As president of the organization, Mr. Doyle wrote "A Manifesto of Men's Liberation" which states the position of the M.R.A. on several issues, most notably the unfairness of the courts and laws toward men. The following viewpoint is taken from that Manifesto.

As you read, consider the following questions:

1. Mr. Doyle says that men are severely discriminated against in several important areas. What, according to him, are the primary causes of this?
2. What are the two areas Mr. Doyle is most concerned about? What evidence does he cite of anti-male discrimination?
3. Does Mr. Doyle see any solutions to the problems he describes? If so, what?

R.F. Doyle, "A Manifesto of Men's Liberation," 2nd edition, Men's Rights Association, P.O. Box 189, Forest Lake, MN 55025, 1980. Reprinted with permission.

Objective examination demonstrates that over the past 30 years anti-male discrimination has become far greater, in scope, in degree and in damage, than any which may exist against women. It takes the form of violations of law, decency and common sense that can be described as unconscionable at best. It is most evident in the areas of domestic relations, employment, and crime and punishment, and denigration of the very male image itself.

The social repercussions are predictable and catastrophic. They include:

a. The male image is becoming that of "Jack-the-Ripper" or "Dagwood Bumstead."

b. The female image is emerging supreme, almost to the point of canonization.

c. Women and bureaucracies are usurping male roles and functions in family and industry.

d. The sexes are becoming indistinguishable. More and more persons are becoming sexual nonentities and homosexuals.

e. Fifty percent of marriages end in divorce.

f. A large percentage of children therefore are being deprived of normal family lives, due to divorce.

g. Defeated, emasculated men, in ever-increasing numbers, are matriculating into the flotsam and jetsam of skid row.

h. Immorality, neurotic instability, drug addiction, delinquency, crime, and other aberrations are being spawned at a disasterous rate.

i. The resultant welfare, corrections and mental institution burdens are becoming staggering, actually, intolerable . . . .

We have attempted to identify the causes. Summarized, they seem to be: distortion of sexual identity and function, displacement and subordination of the male, a perversion of chivalry, and plain old greed . . . .

A "Sacred Cow" syndrome regarding women permeates our society. An example is the great concern in wars and disasters over the killing and maiming of women and children. The killing and maiming of men is of less, if any, importance.

Men are treated like second class citizens throughout the entire spectrum of crime and punishment. Operating under the assumption that two wrongs make a right, government, business and industry discriminate against men in employment and promotion through "Affirmative Action" programs.

The roles of family provider, protector, disciplinarian, and co-rearer of children, traditionally within the functions of husband and father, are being usurped by women, by the welfare department, by other agencies and by the legal fraternity.

Governmental Responsibility

The foregoing philosophies, and the more vicious anti-male attitudes covered later, have been assimilated by government offices. Government employees, from judges to legal aid lawyers, are like self-appointed Galahads, who can't, or don't, distinguish between ladies and women. They eagerly welcome opportunities to rescue damsels in distress and to enforce men's responsibilities. Men's rights must be purchased by hiring expensive lawyers....

Probably the most extensive and outrageous manifestation of anti-male prejudice is in divorce....Divorce courts are frequently like slaughter-houses, with about as much compassion and talent. They function as collection agencies for lawyer fees, however outrageous, stealing children and extorting money from men in ways blatantly unconstitutional. Job havens for the incompetent and catchpolls, the arrogance and archaic mentalities permeating so many are unspeakable. Men are regarded as mere guests in their homes, evictable any time at the whims of wives and judges. Men are driven from home and children against their wills, then when unable to stretch paychecks far enough to support two households are termed "runaway fathers." Contrary to all principles of justice, men are thrown into prison for inability to pay alimony and support, however unreasonable or unfair the "obligation." Dispel all notion that written "law" controls divorce. It has very little impact. Indeed, few judges are even aware of statutory provisions. Judicial whim, or (to grant the pretense of respectability) "discretion", is the actual basis on which decisions are made. Recourse to legal remedies is practically non-existent.

In custody and property disposition morality and fitness are insignificant. Sex-gender is the primary criteria. Women, regardless of merit— whether they're unstable, tramps, lesbians, or whatever, are routinely awarded almost everything—especially custody of children (in 95% of cases) and continuing financial sustenance....

"YOU'RE WELL QUALIFIED FOR THE JOB, MR. WIMBISH, BUT SEEING OUR COMPANY DOESN'T DISCRIMINATE BY SEX IN HIRING WE'RE LOOKING FOR A WOMAN TO FILL IT."

The next largest area of male subordination is crime and punishment; from decision to arrest, amount of bail required, guilt or innocence in judgement, severity of sentences, physical conditions of imprisonment, to release on parole.

Men are jailed on offenses for which women would be winked at. They receive stiffer sentences for similar, or lesser, crimes than women. For example, if a man looks into a home in which a woman is undressing, he will be arrested for window peeping. Reverse the situation, with the woman looking in, again the man will be arrested—this time for indecent exposure. Women are murdering husbands or boyfriends and getting off scott-free, by simply pleading "brutality." It's a near epidemic. Often the victims were sound asleep or even living separately. That these women could simply pack up and leave doesn't even occur to the courts. On the other hand, men may receive 50 year sentences for rapes wherein the victim suffers no physical damage. Contrast the sentences received by Patti Hearst and William James Runnel (whose life sentence by the State of Texas for theft of $299.11 was upheld by the U.S. Supreme Court) and Robert Earl May Jr. (a 14 year old Brookhaven, Mass. boy who got 48 years for armed robbery). Men's Rights Ass'n files are bursting with such examples.

Consider how many men are in jail as opposed to women. According to a recent survey by the U.S. Law Enforcement Assistance Administration, 94% of prisoners are male. Does anyone suggest this to be the proportion of evil in men to that in women? Consider the condition of men's prisons vis a vis those of women's prisons. The former are like dungeons, with cages of steel and concrete. The latter are usually like campuses, with furnished, TV-equipped cottages and grounds for strolling....

Women's Lib

Normal women are the most pampered creatures in western society. In fact, bluntly put, many are parasites, living off the production of men and doing little more to justify their existence than cooking and cleaning a few hours a week, and perhaps computing the value of these services as if the husband were the only beneficiary. This is called biting the hand that feeds you. The alleged discrimination against women in employment, abortion, and miscellaneous areas is insignificant compared to that against men in crime and punishment, employment, and domestic relations. Braying, irrational, but widely heard neo-feminists are cluttering the women's cause with emotional trash, non-issues, impractical solutions and some dangerous policies. They need only perch glasses atop their head and babble "newspeak." People, especially the liberal press, take them seriously....

The very term, "feminists," is misleading. Most adherents are attempting to destroy all traces of feminity. Hence we shall term them "neo-feminists."

Neo-feminists demand to become employed at work men can do best in numbers equal to their population. Government and industry,

85

taking the line of least resistance, are giving women preference in hiring and promotion, regardless of qualification. This is causing hardship to male family breadwinners, especially the emerging Blacks. The military and police forces are becoming weakened by an influx of women, seriously threatening this country's security. Yet not one neo-feminist in a hundred is prepared to sacrifice the privileges routinely accorded women by virtue of their sex, or to demand equal treatment with men in the areas where men are discriminated against. One never sees them clamoring for the dirty jobs men must perform or for equal representation in jails or skid row. It's a "have their cake and eat it too" situation . . . .

But this is not to imply that all blame lies on the shoulders of women, judges, lawyers and institutions. Males themselves are largely responsible for allowing this sorry condition to develop, by gradually surrendering their rights, shirking their responsibilities and abdicating their trousers. Fuzzy-headed housemales, purporting to represent "men's liberation," but sponsored by NOW, are denouncing their masculinity while groping at each other in "consciousness raising" sessions. The bleats of these eunuchs have been hailed as representative of men's liberation. Nothing could be further from the truth . . . . Men's liberation means establishing the right of males to *be men*; not to liberate them *from being men*.

In the face of their treatment most men lie down and roll over in the manner of submissive dogs. This only encourages further tyranny. Protest must be made. Male dignity and men's rights must be restored, preserved and protected against the excesses of society, legalists, and bureaucrats. Just and competent administration of law must be implemented.

"Men are the only sex whose brutalization is still a legitimate form of entertainment."

Men Need Liberating from the Double Standard

Fredric Hayward

Fredric Hayward is the national director of Men's Rights, Inc., an organization concerned with equal rights for men and women. Mr. Hayward has written numerous articles related to this issue. In this viewpoint he reflects on an episode of violence and argues that society has become accustomed to male "brutalization."

As you read, consider the following questions:
1. What is the "double standard" mentioned in the article?
2. How, according to the author, do women participate in the exploitation of men?
3. Why, according to the author, are men victims of society?

Reprinted by permission of author.

It was a case of violence in a neighborhood bar. Someone was physically threatened in front of a crowd of patrons. No one called the police, some because they did not want to get involved, many because they wanted to watch.

The entertainment began. The crowd cheered. Gasped. Cheered again. Someone whose mistake was to be in the wrong place at the wrong time was being seriously hurt.

Then it was over. The animated crowd drifted back to their drinking. In conversation, they relived the highlights of the event. Some patrons went home. All were satisfied. Except for one suffering person who will be lucky to recover from this brutality in a few months. Of course, the emotional injury probably will last longer than the physical one.

The victim of this barroom brutality was a man. (Sorry. Did you think I was talking about a different incident?) How many men this happens to has never been counted. The police do not categorize these assaults, and most are never reported.

Fight Promotion

It can begin in a number of ways. A woman at the bar rejects a man's advances; he picks a fight to salvage his masculine pride. Or one man does not like the race, politics, hairstyle or favorite basketball team of another man. Or some woman wants to be assured that she is attractive enough, or loved enough, to be fought over. Or a local gang wants to experience the togetherness that comes with beating up an outsider. Or a woman wants to exercise power over a bigger animal, so she looks to the bouncer or other hero to push around a man who offends her. Fighting is a male role, but fight promotion is an equal opportunity.

The movement to free us from traditional sex roles has yet to develop a respectable way for a man to avoid fighting. The cheering crowd and the silent witnesses give the aggressor a free hand. The victim knows that he probably cannot get away, and if he did, he could never return with his head up. Take your beating like a man, and do not expect people to march in the streets to protest your treatment.

When a woman is raped, some people have the nerve to suggest that she deserved it. When a man is attacked, most people will suggest that he did deserve it. The people who say "don't blame the victim" are talking about female victims. Those who condemn sexist stereotyping often are careful to ignore the sexist stereotypes that serve their bias.

A rare variation on barroom brutality happened last month in New Bedford, Mass. It was rare because a woman was the victim, and it was a woman's suffering that provided the entertainment. It was rare also because people were horrified enough to protest by the thousands.

Men's Brutalization

I have a fantasy that someday people will become so outraged over

88

a men's issue that they protest on behalf of men. It does not matter which of the many men's issues draws that attention—that only men are still required by law to carry out traditional sex roles; that only men are forbidden by law to make a decision about parenthood after a child is conceived; that only men are expected to give their lives in combat; that only men are subjected at birth to painful and unnecessary surgery; or that men are the only sex whose brutalization is still a legitimate form of entertainment.

Ironically, feminist demands to be treated as equal with men and feminist demands to curtail violence against women are mutually ex-

"How d'yer feel about being 'liberated' so you can run after bloodthirsty animals with this home-made spear?"

clusive. If men stopped sacrificing their own safety for that of a woman, if there were as much honor in beating up a woman as in beating up a man, and if the obligation to defend the nation fell on women as well as men, the double standard might be sorely missed.

"The nature of masculinity is such that the male is unable even to recognize that he is in hazard."

Men Need Liberating from Masculine Myths

Herb Goldberg

Born in Berlin, Germany, Herb Goldberg received his Ph.D. from Adelphi University in 1963. A practicing psychotherapist and Professor of Psychology at California State University in Los Angeles, he has contributed to numerous professional publications. He has also written several popular books, two on the plight of contemporary men. Dr. Goldberg's most recent book is *The New Male-Female Relationship* (1983). In the viewpoint below Dr. Goldberg discusses some of the harmful "myths of masculinity" from which he believes men must free themselves.

As you read, consider the following questions:

1. What are the characteristics of the "myths of masculinity" that Dr. Goldberg deplores? Why are these traits potentially dangerous to men?
2. What potential for men does Dr. Goldberg see in the women's liberation movement?
3. What does Dr. Goldberg mean by his opening statement, "Women bend and men break"?

Women bend and men break. The blueprint for masculinity is a blueprint for self-destruction. It is a process so deeply embedded in the male consciousness, however, that awareness of its course and its end has been lost. The masculine imperative, the pressure and compulsion to perform, to prove himself, to dominate, to live up to the "masculine ideal"—in short, to "be a man"—supersedes the instinct to survive. His psychological fragility and volatility may even cause him to destroy a lifetime of work and relationships in a momentary impulse.

The diagnosis of chauvinism is superficial. More often it is a gross and misleading distortion. Closer examination of a man's behavior reveals a powerfully masochistic, self-hating and often pathetically self-destructive style.

The brittle male conducts his life by his *ideas* about masculinity. Living up to the *image* is the important thing. Though the moment-to-moment experience may be painful and generally unsatisfying for him, his mind is continually telling him *what he is supposed to be*. As long as he is able to be that way, he can fend off the inner demons that threaten him with accusations of not being "a man".

As his isolation and distrust, the hallmarks of "successful" masculinity, increase, so do his drive for power and control and his inner rage and frustration. He senses the human experience drifting beyond his reach forever. By trying to control the world, even "improve" it or change it, he may simply be trying to make it a place in which he can safely become human—more loving and less aggressive. But the plan fails. His great hunger to prove himself, plus his anger and distrust, drive the possibilities of intimacy away. As his life unfolds and he is well into living up to masculine expectations, his behavior and choices for emotional nourishment may very well become more desperate and bizarre.

Driven by Idea of Manhood

Traditional masculinity is largely a psychologically defensive operation rather than an authentic and organic process. A man's psychological energy is used to defend *against*, rather than to express, what he really is. His efforts are directed at proving to himself and others what *he is not*: feminine, dependent, emotional, passive, afraid, helpless, a loser, a failure, impotent and so on. He burns himself out in this never-ending need to prove, because he can *never* sufficiently prove it. To his final day he is driven to project himself as "a man," whether on the battlefield, behind the desk, in lovemaking, on the hospital operating table, in a barroom or even on his deathbed. And when he fails, his self-hate and humiliation overwhelm him.

He would sooner die than acknowledge the things that threaten him most. And yet his deepest imprint is feminine, for it was a woman, not a man, who was his lifeline and his deepest source of identification when he was a baby and a young boy. The femininity is therefore naturally a part of his core. The stronger that identification is and the

91

more it threatens, the more powerfully will he need to deny it. Prisons, as well as violent street gangs, are filled with men who have "Mother" tattooed on their arm. . . .

In the traditional contemporary American home, the feminine imprint is particularly deep because the father sees himself as an incompetent, bumbling parent whose only legitimate territory is the office or the factory. He defers to the innate "maternal wisdom" of his wife in the early child-rearing process. Or he is by necessity simply minimally present, consumed by economic pressures. He is a father in name rather than in behavior, his role is to keep the bills paid and provide for the necessities of life. In many cases, divorce has made him largely a stranger to his family.

A Real Man

Real Men have always lived by one simple rule: never settle with words what you can accomplish with a flame thrower.

But if you want to see what's happening to us now, look at today's movies. Instead of having John Wayne fight Nazis and Commies for peace and democracy, we've got Dustin Hoffman fighting Meryl Streep for a six-year-old in *Kramer vs. Kramer.* It's no wonder things are so mixed up. Thirty years ago the Duke would have slapped the broad around and shipped the kid off to military school. Not anymore. I'm convinced things were better in the past.

All a Real Man had to do was abuse women, steal land from Indians and find some place to dump toxic waste. . . .Now you're expected to be sympathetic, sensitive and to split the household chores.

Bruce Feinstein, *Real Men Don't Eat Quiche*, New York: Pocket Books, 1981, from *Reader's Digest,* Dec. '82.

The emotions are there, but the admonitions against expressing them have progressively caused them to be blocked out of consciousness. As a boy the message he received was clear: Feelings are taboo.

Repression of Feelings

Recently I conducted a marathon therapy group for married couples in a small city in the Midwest, where most of the men still behave in gender-traditional ways. I began by asking each man to write about his feelings, about his life as it was for him, and about his marriage. Five of the eight men insisted that they had *no feelings* inside themselves at all. With assistance, they eventually began to get in touch with their emotions, and it was not hard to understand why they had been blocked. Feelings of frustration, resentment, conflict, loneliness and of not being cared for lay underneath. The men were afraid of these emotions and would not know how to deal with them if they acknowledged them. On the surface, in self-protection, all of these men were "macho"—detached, hyperrational and tough—in short, machinelike. Of course, all of them drank before coming home each day after work, and heavily on weekends. They were burning out rapidly in every way.

The feminist movement has brought the man's rigidity forth in maximal relief. If his fear of change weren't so powerful, he would embrace the movement for the lifegiving and life-expanding possibilities it offers him: a release from age-old guilt and responsibility toward women and from many onerous burdens. And if he could redefine himself and perceive women differently, he could begin to achieve the rebirth in heterosexual relationships that would come from equal responsibility and comfortable self-expression. However, unable to change, he is afraid of women's changing, too. As a result of his rigidity, the transformation in women only spells danger in the form of abandonment and potential emotional starvation.

It is my interpretation that on the deepest archetypal level the feminist movement is partially fueled by an intuitive sensing of the decay and demise of the male. Women are rushing in to take men's places, as much for survival's sake as for any sociological or philosophical reasons. He has become a hyperactive, hyper-cerebral, hyper-mechanical, rigid, self-destructive machine out of control.

In 1910 there were 106.2 men for every 100 women in the population at large. By 1970, about the time when the feminist movement began to develop momentum, there were approximately 94.8 men for every 100 women. In 1978, by age sixty-five, there were only 75 men left for every 100 women. Little boys fall prey to major illnesses, such as hyperkinesis, autism, stuttering and so on, at rates several hundred percent higher than little girls. The suicide rate for men is also several times higher than for women, to say nothing of the many indirect and less obvious ways in which men kill themselves. And the behavior of the up-and-coming generations of men suggests that the self-destructive trend may be accelerating. . . .

Unrecognized Hazard

The nature of masculinity is such that the male is unable even to recognize that he is in hazard. His life seems to him to be totally within his control. Unaccustomed to self-examination, he blocks out awareness of the way he lives and the conditioning that created it. He stoically accepts his lot as a given, or at best a challenge that the "real man" will accept and cope with and only the "sissy" will not. . . .

The repression of emotion, the denial and suppression of vulnerability, the compulsive competitiveness, the fear of losing, the anxiety over touching or any other form of sensual display, the controlled intellectualizing, and the general lack of spontaneity and unselfconscious playfulness serve to make the companionship of most men unsatisfying and highly limited. Men are at their best when a task has to be completed, a problem solved, or an enemy battled. Without such a structure, however, anxiety and self-consciousness accelerate too rapidly to allow for a sustained pleasurable experience.

This is also what makes feminist independence a threat. If a man cannot turn to other men in a crisis; if there is no support available to see him through periods of transition and change; if he can only bond comfortably with other men in pursuit of a tangible goal or to defeat a common enemy, he has no basis of intimacy for reaching out to them. It is particularly uncomfortable in moments of weakness, vulnerability, humiliation or pain.

His relationship with his woman is suffocated by the heavy weight of his dependency and draining demandingness, as he turns to her for everything. If she abandons him, his emotional lifeline will have been cut. At the same time, he never clearly defines what it is that he needs or wants from her. He detaches himself, with occasional moments of explosiveness, to control the torrent of unexpressed feelings. She will in turn either come to hate him for it or "suffer through it" masochistically.

Finally, there will be rapid physical decline, because health-giving things are mainly feminine. To take care is not masculine.

Before the age of liberation and feminism he could rationalize this self-destructiveness: He was doing it for his wife and family. That made it all valid and worthwhile. Today the enlightened and honest woman is owning up. "You're not doing it for me: you're doing it for yourself. And if you're doing it for me, please stop, because I'm not getting anything from it. It's boring. It's dead and I hate it."

But the sham is revealed. In spite of the fact that she no longer wants what he is giving her, he can't stop giving it. . . .

As a cardboard Goliath, the male cannot easily shift direction. It was recently reported by Dr. Sandra Bem, based on her extensive research, that "while high masculinity in males has been related to better psychological adjustment during adolescence, it is often accompanied during adulthood by high anxiety, high neuroticism and low self-acceptance. . . . Boys who are strongly masculine and girls who are strongly feminine tend to have lower overall intelligence, lower spatial ability, and show lower creativity."

If he continues to cling to the traditional masculine blueprint, he will be a victim of himself. He will end his life as a pathetic throwaway, abandoned and asleep.

"Men, I have come to believe, cannot or will not have real friends."

Men Need Liberating from Repressed Feelings

Richard Cohen

Richard Cohen received his Master's Degree in Journalism from Columbia University. He has written for United Press International and for the *Washington Post*. Presently a syndicated columnist for the *Post*, Mr. Cohen's columns are seen in hundreds of newspapers daily. In the following viewpoint, he comments on men's inability to have intimate friends and attributes this to erroneous concepts of what constitutes "manly behavior."

As you read, consider the following questions:
1. What does "friend" seem to mean to Mr. Cohen?
2. What does he think is the reason men do not have friends?

Richard Cohen, "Men Have Buddies, But No Real Friends." © 1983, The Washington Post Company. Reprinted with permission.

My friends have no friends. They are men. They think they have friends, and if you ask them whether they have friends they will say yes, but they don't really. They think, for instance, that I'm their friend, but I'm not. It's OK. They're not my friends either.

The reason for that is that we are all men—and men, I have come to believe, cannot or will not have real friends. They have something else—companions, buddies, pals, chums, someone to drink with and someone to wench with and someone to lunch with, but no one when it comes to saying how they feel—especially how they hurt.

Women know this. They talk about it among themselves. I heard one woman describe men as the true Third World people—still not yet emerged. To women, this inability of men to say what they feel is a source of amazement and then anguish and then, finally, betrayal. Women will tell you all the time that they don't know the men they live with. They talk of long silences and drifting off and of keeping feelings hidden and never letting on that they are troubled or bothered or whatever.

If it's any comfort to women, they should know that it's nothing personal. Men treat other men the same way.

For instance, I know men who have suffered brutal professional setbacks and never mentioned it to their friends. I know of a guy who never told his best friend that his own son had a rare childhood disease. And I know others who never have sex with their wives, but talk to their friends as though they're living in the Playboy Mansion, either pretending otherwise or saying nothing.

This is something men learn early. It is something I learned from my father, who taught me, the way fathers teach sons, to keep my emotions to myself. I watched him and learned from him. One day we went to the baseball game, cheered and ate and drank, and the next day he was taken to the hospital with yet another ulcer attack. He had several of them. My mother said he worried a lot, but I saw none of this.

Legend has it that men talk a lot about sex. They don't. They talk about it only in the sense that it is treated like sports. They joke about it and rate women from one to 10. But they almost never talk about it in a way that matters—the quality of it. They almost never talk in real terms, in terms other than a cartoon, in terms that apply to them and the woman or women with whom they have a relationship.

A Lesson from Women

Women do talk that way. Women talk about fulfillment, and they admit—maybe complain is the better word—to nonexistent sex lives. No man would admit to virtually having no sex life, yet there are plenty who do.

When I was a kid, I believed that it was men who had real friend-ships and women who did not. This seemed to be the universal belief, and boys would talk about this. We wondered about girls, about what made them so catty that they could not have friendships, and we really

96

thought we were lucky to be men and have real friends.

We thought our friendships would last forever; we talked about them in some sort of Three Musketeer fashion—all for one and one for all. If one of us needed help, all of us would come running. We are still friends, some of us, anyway, and I still feel that I will fight for them, but I don't think I could confide in them. No—not that.

Richard Cohen

Sometimes I think that men are walking relics—outmoded and out-dated, programed for some other age. We have all the essential qualities for survival in the wild and for success in battle, but we run like hell from talking about our feelings. We are, as the poet said in a different context, truly a thing of wonder.

Some women say that they have always had this ability to confide in one another—to talk freely. Others say that this is something relatively new—yet another benefit of the woman's movement. I don't

97

know. All I know is that they have it, and most men don't, and even the men who do—the ones who can talk about how they feel—talk to women. Have we been raised to think of feelings and sentiment as feminine? Can a man talk intimately with another man and not wonder about his masculinity? I don't know. I do know it sometimes makes the other men feel uncomfortable.

I know this is a subject that concerns me, and yet I find myself bottling it all up—keeping it all in. I've been on automatic pilot for years now.

The Best of Friends

There is nothing among men that resembles the personal communication that women have developed among themselves. . . .

We are taught not to communicate our personal feelings and concerns.

Looking back, I realize that my only points of contact with one of my closest friends of several years ago were playing poker and tennis together, eating dinners cooked by his wife, and rehashing the Vietnam war and other "large" problems. Never anything personal. . .

Talking personally and spontaneously involves revealing doubts, plans which may fail, ideas which haven't been thought through, happiness over things the other person may think trivial—in short, making ourselves vulnerable. That was too risky.

The most painful thing, in retrospect, is that we thought we were the best of friends.

Marc Fasteau, "Why Aren't We Talking?" *MS.*, July, 1972.

It would be nice to break out of it. It would be nice to join the rest of the human race, connect with others in a way that makes sense, in a way that's meaningful—in a way that's more than a dirty joke and a slap on the back. I wonder whether it can be done.

If it can, it will happen because women will insist on it, because they themselves have shown the way, come out of the closet as women, talked about it, organized, defined an agenda, set their goals and admitted that as women—just as women—they have problems in common. So do men. It's time to talk about them.

"When too many men are subverted, the society itself is jeopardized."

Men Need Liberating from Women's Liberation

George F. Gilder

Author of several well-received books on sociological topics, George F. Gilder received his A.B. degree from Harvard University in 1962. He has been an editor and political speechwriter and is currently on the editorial board of *National Review*. His most recent book is *Wealth and Poverty* (1981). The viewpoint below is taken from Mr. Gilder's 1973 work, *Sexual Suicide*. In it he argues that women's liberationists endanger society because, in challenging traditional sex roles they challenge the whole function of males. If men do not maintain their dominance, they, and therefore society, will be destroyed.

As you read, consider the following questions:
1. Mr. Gilder says that men are innately inferior to women—in what way?
2. The author writes that it is vital to society to keep men happy, productive, and self-satisfied. Why? And how can society best achieve this?
3. What do you think of Mr. Gilder's rationale for keeping men in higher-paying and higher-status jobs?

The chief perpetrators of [society's] problems are men: Men commit over 90 percent of major crimes of violence, 100 percent of the rapes, 95 percent of the burglaries. They comprise 94 percent of our drunken drivers, 70 percent of suicides, 91 percent of offenders against family and children. More specifically, the chief perpetrators are *single* men. Single men comprise between 80 and 90 percent of most of the categories of social pathology, and on the average they make less money than any other group in the society—yes, less than single women or married women. As any insurance actuary will tell you, single men are also less responsible about their bills, their driving, and other personal conduct. Together with the disintegration of the family, they constitute our leading social problem. For there has emerged no institution that can replace the family in turning children into civilized human beings or in retrieving the wreckage of our current disorder.

Yet what is our leading social movement? It's Women's Liberation, with a whole array of nostrums designed to emancipate us. From what? From the very institution that is most indispensable to overcoming our present social crisis: the family . . . .

Sexuality, family unity, kinship, masculine solidarity, maternity, motivation, nurturing, all the rituals of personal identity and development, all the bonds of community, seem "sexist," "superstitious," "mystical," "inefficient," "discriminatory." And, of course, they are—and they are also indispensable to a civilized society . . . .

Sex Differences

[Anthropologist] Margaret Mead says it best: "If any human society—large or small, simple or complex, based on the most rudimentary hunting and fishing, or on the whole elaborate interchange of manufactured products—is to survive, it must have a pattern of social life that comes to terms with the differences between the sexes . . . .

Apart from the diversity of mankind, this is perhaps the clearest lesson of the anthropologist. How a tribe manages its sexuality—its births, matings, kinship ties—determines the nature of the tribe and its durability . . . .

One of the concerns of every society is how to respond to the essentially unprogrammed form of male sexual energy . . . .

A man who is oriented toward a family he loves—or wants to create—is apt to work more consistently and productively than a man oriented toward his next fix, lay, day at the races, or drinking session with the boys. A man who feels affirmed sexually by his work environment, and his relation to other men and women in it, will produce more than a man who finds his job sexually erosive and confusing. A man who is integrated into a community through a role in a family, spanning generations into the past and future, will be more consistently and durably tied to the social order than a man responding chiefly to a charismatic leader, a demagogue, or a grandiose ideology of patriotism....

A man's commitments to his job, his career, his family—his deferred gratifications and his sacrifices for the larger community—are not the product of a simple calculus of costs and benefits. Rather this behavior pattern is motivated by a system of sexual relationships and affirmations.... Crucial is the desire, conscious or unconscious, for progeny with a specific woman, who subjects the male's sexual drive to long-term female patterns.

Because the father's role is a cultural invention rather than a biological imperative, however, the civilizing impulse of love is psychologically fragile. The subordination of male sexual rhythms to the long-term cycles of female sexuality is constantly subject to erosion by short term male impulses: to give up the job, the family, and pursue a life of immediate gratification. The husband's commitment thus needs external props.

Loosening the Family Bond

While the language of lib emphasizes "equality" and "freedom," what is actually occurring at the psychological and social levels is the breakdown of the sense of commitment and duty that husbands and wives, parents and children, feel for one another. This begins with feminists who try to destroy the confidence of women in the protections of marriage and the security and value of their wifely status in the home. Once the wife is persuaded to shift the focus of her life away from home, husband and children, the sense of mutual commitment between family members tends to evaporate as they come to spend little time together and the home becomes less significant as a primary focus of concern and sustenance. As the wife withdraws her confidence in the husband as breadwinner and protector, he in turn often feels less called upon to perform traditional duties, and gradually the sense of living with a group of independent agents affects everyone.

Jim Fordham "with his indispensable wife Andrea," *The Assault on the Sexes*, New Rochelle, NY: Arlington House, Publishers, 1977.

The sexual constitution has long afforded three principal props. The first is the insistence of most women on some degree of monogamy. In general, a man still cannot get sex easily and dependably with women he likes unless he foregoes others, or undertakes some deceitful drama of love that is a strain on his conscience. The second support is marriage. The culture still exalts it with religious ceremony and affirms it with legal sanctions and social pressures. Third is the male role as the essential provider. This gives the man a position in wedlock to some extent commensurate with the woman's. Otherwise he is inferior. In social terms the family is formed to create a stable home for children. The woman's role is clearly indispensable while the man's is secondary. The whole sexual constitution is based on

101

the maternal tie. . . .

Paternity, as a cultural invention, will not serve to give the man a durable role in the family; and there is virtually no society that successfully relies on it to keep the man actively present. To keep the man present and to preserve the nuclear family as the prevailing institution, even love will not long suffice. He must be needed in a practical and material way. . . .

Job and Money Roles

In these terms, the sexual role of most jobs is far more important than their economic function. In its extraordinary complexity, modern civilization is also extremely vulnerable to the outlaw—whether the alcoholic driver or the hijacker, the guerrilla or the drug addict, the mugger or the assassin.

The real contribution made by individual men in their work rarely exceeds the real damage they can do if their masculinity is not socialized or subjected to female patterns. . . .

Crucial to the sexual constitution of employment is that, in one way or another, it assures that over the whole society, class by class, most men will make more money than most women. . . . In essence, the additional pay is part of a tacit social contract by which men are induced to repress antisocial patterns. On the immediate and superficial level, justice and efficiency—so stressed by the feminists—have little to do with it. . . .

Equality Leads to Superiority

Suffer women once to arrive at equality with you, and they will from that moment on become your superiors.

Cato the Elder, 195 B.C.

A male's money is socially affirmative. If the man is unmarried, a much higher proportion of his money than a woman's will be spent on the opposite sex. His money gives him the wherewithal to make long-term sexual initiatives. It gives him the courage to submit to female sexual patterns, for he knows he will retain the crucial role of familial support. His sexual impulses can assume the civilizing rather than the subversive form. . . .

The [women's] movement is striking at the Achilles' heel of civilized society: the role of the male. They are correct that it is a cultural contrivance and that it can be destroyed. But they are wrong to suppose that men, shorn of their current schemes of socialization, would mildly accept the new roles provided by the movement. New roles can work only if they come to terms with the sexual inferiority and compensatory aggressiveness of the male, only if they afford a distinctive male identity that accords with the special predicament of male sexuality in civilized society.

102

"Patriarchy is universal... There has never been a society that has failed to associate authority and leadership... with men."

The Dominant Male Needs No Liberating

Steven Goldberg

Steven Goldberg has taught sociology at the City College of New York. He has contributed to numerous professional periodicals. In 1973, his book *The Inevitability of Patriarchy*, from which this viewpoint is taken, argued that it is absolutely inevitable that men be the dominant members of society. Even if society changed the traditional male and female functions, he says, the male roles, whatever they might be, would become the higher status and more powerful roles.

As you read, consider the following questions:
1. What is patriarchy?
2. In every society, according to Dr. Goldberg, male tasks, whether they be cooking or hunting, building or babysitting, teaching or lawyering, have higher status than female tasks. Why?
3. Dr. Goldberg sees *one* disadvantage to the way nature has set up male and female roles. What is it?

Patriarchy is any system of organization (political, economic, religious, or social) that associates authority and leadership primarily with males and in which males fill the vast majority of authority and leadership positions. . . . Patriarchy is universal. For all the variety different societies have demonstrated in developing different types of political, economic, religious, and social systems, there has never been a society that has failed to associate authority and leadership in these areas with men. No anthropologist contests the fact that patriarchy is universal. Indeed, of all social institutions there is probably none whose universality is so totally agreed upon. While I think it fair to say that most anthropologists consider the family, marriage, and the incest taboo universal—and believe that, while it is easy to *imagine* societies without one or more of these institutions, no real society could survive without them—with each of these institutions anthropologists debate problems of definition and borderline cases. There is not, nor has there ever been, any society that even remotely failed to associate authority and leadership in suprafamilial areas with the male. . . .

There have been three cases of women attaining the highest positions of authority in democracies (Israel, India, and Ceylon), though in the latter two instances the woman was the daughter and widow, respectively, of a revered man and it is hardly likely that either would have otherwise attained power. The point of importance, however, is that even in such societies authority has continued to be overwhelmingly associated with the male and the overwhelming number of positions of leadership have been filled by men. In Israel, for example, the other eighteen ministerial positions are filled by men and the proportion of men at each level of the hierarchy of political authority is roughly the same as it is in the United States, Sweden, Cuba, Communist China, and the Soviet Union.

Male Dominance

Male dominance refers to the *feeling* acknowledged by the emotions of both men and women that the woman's will is somehow subordinate to the male's and that general authority . . . ultimately resides in the male. . . . As was the case with patriarchy, male dominance is universal; no society has ever failed to conform its expectations of men and women, and the social roles relevant to these expectations, to the feeling of men and women that it is the male who "takes the lead." Every society accepts the existence of these feelings, and conforms to their existence by socializing children accordingly, because every society must. . . .

In every society, whatever the particular tasks performed by women, the members feel that women do "women's tasks" (as defined by the particular society) either because only women are biologically capable of the tasks or because men serve functions that are more crucial to the society's survival. *Every society gives higher status to male roles than to the nonmaternal roles of females.* To put it another, and

I believe more illuminating way: *in every society males attain the high-status (nonmaternal) roles and positions and perform the high-status tasks, whatever those tasks are . . .*

Margaret Mead has written:

> In every known human society, the male's need for achievement can be recognized. *Men may cook, or weave or dress dolls or hunt hummingbirds, but if such activities are appropriate occupations of men, then the whole society, men and women alike, votes them as important. When the same occupations are performed by women, they are regarded as less important.* [Emphasis added]

A woman who is older, wealthier, from a higher class or "better" family, more intelligent, or more educated than a particular male may be given authority over that male and perhaps she may even feel dominance over him, but she will have less status and authority than an equivalent male and she will feel deference toward him. Thus in some societies the older woman whose husband has died rules the family, and the presence of an educated, wealthy woman will make the less wealthy and educated male experience feelings of insecurity. *But whatever variable one chooses, authority, status, and dominance within each stratum rest with the male in contacts with equivalent females.*

Steven Goldberg

Men do not merely fill most of the roles in high-status areas, they also fill the high-status roles in low-status areas. The higher the level of power, authority, status, prestige, or position—whether the area be economic, occupational, political, or religious—the higher the percentage of males. Thus the percentage of women in the work force in the United States has risen by 75 percent since 1900, but the percentage of women in the high-status area of medicine has declined during this period. In the Soviet Union, where medicine has a far lower status than it does in the United States, the majority of all doctors are women, but as one ascends from the level of practical medicine to the levels of authority the percentage of males rises until, at the top, males constitute the overwhelming majority.

Of all the *tasks* one might think of or choose to emphasize, virtually every one, with the exception of those related to protection, fighting, and political authority, is associated with women in one society or another, but in every society it is the roles filled by men that are given high status....

At the bottom of it all man's job is to protect woman and woman's is to protect her infant; in nature all else is luxury. There are feminists who try to have it both ways; they deny the importance of the biological basis of the behavior of the sexes, yet blame the world's woes on the male characteristics of its leaders. The latter hypothesis is correct, and we find that we are trapped in what could be the final irony: the biological factors that underlie women's life-sustaining abilities—the qualities most vital to the survival of our species—preclude women's ever manifesting the psychological predisposition, the obsessive need of power, or the abilities necessary for the attainment of significant amounts of political power....

Women Are Never Equal

Let us be done forever with this nonsense about the equality of the sexes. They are not equal in nature and never can be. If the woman argues—and it is proverbially useless to argue with her—that she wants a chance to show what she can do, the answer is, Certainly, madame, all the chance in the world, for you, and for the man and for the child, opportunity for everybody to cultivate the best that is in him or her for the good of the individual, for the good of the race. But in heaven's name let not women hope to compete with man, for the more chance she has, the freer the world grows, the more chance man will have, and he will always keep slightly ahead of her.

John Macy, *About Women*, New York, Morrow, 1930.

For all the injustices committed in attempts to enforce bogus biological laws, roles associated with gender have been primarily the result rather than the cause of sexual differences. Sex is the single most decisive determinant of personal identity; it is the first thing we notice about another person and the last thing we forget. Just as it is criminal for others to limit one's identity by invoking arbitrary limitations in the name of nature, so it is terribly self-destructive to refuse to accept one's own nature and the joys and powers it invests....

The evidence indicates that women follow their own physiological imperatives and that they would not choose to compete for the goals that men devote their lives to attaining. Women have more important things to do. Men are aware of this and that is why in this and every other society they look to women for gentleness, kindness, and love, for refuge from a world of pain and force, for safety from their own excesses. In every society a basic male motivation is the feeling that the women and children must be protected. But the feminist cannot have it both ways: if she wishes to sacrifice all this, all that she will get in return is the right to meet men on male terms. She will lose.

Recognizing Statements
That Are Provable

From various sources of information we are constantly confronted with statements and generalizations about social and moral problems. In order to think clearly about these problems, it is useful if one can make a basic distinction between statements for which evidence can be found and other statements which cannot be verified or proved because evidence is not available, or the issue is so controversial that it cannot be definitely proved.

Readers should constantly be aware that magazines, newspapers and other sources often contain statements of a controversial nature. The following activity is designed to allow experimentation with statements that are provable and those that are not.

The following statements are taken from the viewpoints in this chapter. Consider each statement carefully. *Mark P for any statement you believe is provable. Mark U for any statement you feel is unprovable because of the lack of evidence. Mark C for statements you think are too controversial to be proved to everyone's satisfaction.*

If you are doing this activity as the member of a class or group, compare your answers with those of other class or group members. Be able to defend your answers. You may discover that others will come to different conclusions than you. Listening to the reasons others present for their answers may give you valuable insights in recognizing statements that are provable.

If you are reading this book alone, ask others if they agree with your answers. You too will find this interaction very valuable.

P = provable
U = unprovable
C = too controversial

1. There is not, nor has there ever been, any society that even remotely failed to associate authority and leadership in suprafamilial areas with the male.

2. Every society gives higher status to male roles than to the non-maternal roles of females.

3. Sex is the single most decisive determinant of personal identity.

4. Men commit over 90 percent of major crimes of violence, 100 percent of the rapes, 95 percent of the burglaries.

5. How a tribe manages its sexuality—its births, mating, kinship ties—determines the nature of the tribe and its durability.

6. Particularly in relatively poor communities, a woman with more money than the men around her tends to demoralize and subvert them.

7. In the typical American home, the feminine imprint is particularly deep because the father sees himself as an incompetent, bumbling parent whose only legitimate territory is the office or the factory.

8. In 1910 there were 106.2 men for every 100 women in the population at large.

9. The suicide rate for men is several times higher than for women, to say nothing of the many indirect and less obvious ways in which men kill themselves.

10. Boys who are strongly masculine and girls who are strongly feminine tend to have lower overall intelligence, lower spatial ability, and show lower creativity.

11. Objective examination demonstrates that over the past 30 years anti-male discrimination has become far greater, in scope, in degree and in damage, than any which may exist against women.

12. As far as divorce courts are concerned, men are regarded as mere guests in their own home, evictable any time at the whims of wives and judges.

13. Men receive stiffer sentences for similar, or lesser, crimes than women.

14. Men's prisons are like dungeons, with cages of steel and concrete. Women's prisons are usually like campuses, with furnished, TV-equipped cottages and grounds for strolling.

15. The alleged discrimination against women in employment, abortion, and miscellaneous areas is insignificant compared to that against men in crime and punishment, employment, and domestic relations.

16. Men have all the essential qualities for survival in the wild and for success in battle, but we run like hell from talking about our feelings.

Bibliography

The following list of periodical articles deals with the subject matter of this chapter.

Francis Baumli   "Men's and Women's Liberation—a Common Cause," *The Humanist*, July/August 1980.

David Behrens   "What Do Men Really Want?" *Glamour*, June 1982.

Robert Brannon   **"Inside the Men's Movement,"** *Ms.*, **October 1982.**

Richard H. Davis   "Self-Assessment at Mid-Life: A Male Crisis," *USA Today*, January 1983.

Steve Ditlea   "In Defense of Macho," *Mademoiselle*, July 1974.

Dollars & Sense   "Wealth and Women—How to Get One at the Expense of the Other," November 1981.

Barbara Ehrenreich   "The Male Revolt," *Mother Jones*, April 1983.

Barbara Ehrenreich   "The Playboy Man and the American Family," *Ms.*, June 1983.

Elliot Engel   "Of Male Bondage," *Newsweek*, June 21, 1982.

Betty Friedan   "Their Turn: How Men Are Changing," *Redbook*, May 1980.

David Gelman & Others   "How Men Are Changing," *Newsweek*, January 16, 1978.

Robert Gould   "Measuring Masculinity by the Size of a Paycheck," *Ms.*, June 1973.

Marvin Harris   "Why Men Dominate Women," *New York Times Magazine*, November 13, 1977.

James Harrison   "Changing Male Roles," *American Education*, July 1977.

B. James   "Have You Ever Wished You Were a Man?" *Mademoiselle*, March 1983.

Julius Lester   "Being a Boy," *Ms.*, July 1973.

Peter McGrath   "Liberation Shock: Are Men Running Scared?" *Mademoiselle*, May 1982.

John Money   "Destereotyping Sex Roles," *Society*, July 1977.

M. Oppenheim   "Men vs. Women: Who's Built Better?" *Mademoiselle*, April 1982.

Reader's Digest   "Are Men Really Changing?" July 1978.

Philip Slater   "Men and Madness: Some Thoughts on the Violence Factor," *Ms.*, October 1982.

Carin Rubenstein   "Real Men Don't Earn Less Than Their Wives," *Psychology Today*, November 1982.

Martin Simmons   "My Main Man! The Truth about Male Friend-ships," *Essense*, November 1981.

Peter Stearns   "We Are Holding on to Male Values That Are Outdated," *U.S. News & World Report*, November 22, 1983.

Doug Thompson   *As Boys Become Men: Learning New Male Roles: Curriculum for Exploring Male Role Stereotyping*, Institute for Equality in Education, University of Colorado, Denver, 1980.

U.S. News & World Report   "Battle of the Sexes—Men Fight Back," December 8, 1980.

Is the Family Obsolete?

*"Women in [America] are increasingly concern-
ed about their own rights and future and
decreasingly concerned about the future of the
family."*

The Family
Is in Danger

David Brudnoy

David Brudnoy is a radio talkshow host on station WRKO in
Boston. In the following viewpoint he voices concern about
current trends in women's attitudes toward marriage and
family.

As you read, consider the following questions:
1. According to Mr. Brudnoy, what conclusions may be drawn
   from the Virginia Slims American Women's Opinion Poll?
2. Why does the author believe that recent changes in attitudes toward marriage and family are polarizing many
   Americans?
3. What characteristics does the author feel contribute to the
   uniqueness of America?

A handsomely produced, thick booklet, looking not surprisingly like a gargantuan cigarette pack, surfaced recently, the gift of the Virginia Slims people. The 1980 Virginia Slims American Women's Opinion Poll conducted by the Roper Organization, offers some surprising views of family life in this country. Roper interviewed 3,000 women and 1,000 men, finding both a wide acceptance of several non-traditional attitudes and practices and a few very traditional attitudes and practices.

While 77 percent of the women interviewed disdain "Ms." and cling happily to "Miss" or "Mrs.," 70 percent of them believe that the institute of marriage has weakened, and with marriage the once almost universally held belief that motherhood and marriage must coincide, preferably, of course, the latter before the former.

The Virginia Slims Poll tells us that 80 percent of the women do not consider children essential to marriage; that 62 percent consider divorce acceptable; that 76 percent approve of abortion; that 51 percent favor the Equal Rights Amendment (vs. 22 percent who oppose, the rest undecided). The gist of the poll is this: those women interviewed seem generally to be more "liberated" from traditional attitudes toward marriage, sex, and the family, even to the point of favoring, by a wide margin, efforts to strengthen the status of women in ways that might well work to weaken the family.

Polarizing Poll

In short, the Virginia Slims American Women's Opinion Poll adds another bit of evidence to the theory that women in this country are increasingly concerned about their own rights and futures and decreasingly concerned about the future of the family.

This cannot help but frighten and anger that large minority of Americans who recoil from recent trends and who wish to, and work

"I'm fed up with being a nuclear family. We should be living in a commune!"

to, counter those trends by accentuating the traditional values. Nor can the Virginia Slims Poll, and many similar statistical data, help but further polarize Americans' attitudes toward the family. Women, and many men, find themselves lining up as if in battle lines, defending their positions as if there could be no possible reconciliation.

And so we hear an increasing stridency in the voices of those women who find virtually the entire thrust of recent changes in our society repugnant. In seeking to "defend" the family they strike out at anybody who diverges from what they consider good and "decent" and right, as if maligning those who have sex before marriage, or who don't care to have children, or who in any of a dozen ways appear to challenge the virtuous self-image of the traditionalists, can rebuild what has been dismantled.

A Siege on Families

The American middle-class family, already stripped of most non-essential duties, now faces an attack on its remaining last bastions. Sex is available premaritally, extra-maritally and non-maritally to more and more Americans. . . .Education has long ago been taken from the family and invested in special institutions, the schools. . . . The rapid rise in women who work. . .or are on welfare, breaks economic dependence as a source of a family bond. . . .

Thus, . . .there is a continued, expanding divesture of missions from the family to other institutions. . . . Nine million children under the age of 18 are being raised by one parent only, mostly by women. . . . According to my calculations, if the present rate of increase in divorce and single households continues to accelerate as it did for the last ten years, by mid-1990 not one American family will be left.

Amitai Etzioni, "The Family: Is It Obsolete?" *Journal of Current Social Issues*, Winter 1977.

And for their part, the champions of the now more trendy ways of life seem to think that only by ridiculing traditional family values can those trendy ways be validated.

Women at War

The result, at least for the moment, is American womanhood at war with itself, and the men find themselves sucked into the fracas, too.

In fact, even while some of these issues are irreconcilable—pro-"choice" and pro-"life" advocates cannot simply split the difference and tromp merrily along, putting the abortion matter behind them—most of these issues are not either-or matters at all. The family can be strengthened without making pariahs of those who can do without it, and new approaches to sexuality for some need not make of the older approach a joke.

It is in our pluralism, our diversity, our ability to encompass many ways of life, that America stands out among nations. The Virginia Slims women indicated that cohabitation would replace marriage (75 percent said this); half felt marriage would "vanish" by the year 2000. I doubt that very much. But marriage will no longer be the future choice of the overwhelming majority of America's women. Still, for those who do choose marriage, and all that has for millenia come with marriage, coexistence with those who choose otherwise is not only possible, it is essential. The times, they are a-changing, but not necessarily into total war.

"One after another, researchers have checked in with news about the tenacity of family life."

The Family Is Strong

Ellen Goodman

Writer Ellen Goodman has worked as a researcher, radio commentator, feature writer, and syndicated columnist. She has also published two books. In 1980 she received a Pulitzer Prize. In the following viewpoint, Ms. Goodman comments on our expectations of family life and the reality of it.

As you read, consider the following questions:
1. What conclusions did sociologist Ted Caplow reach regarding family life in Muncie?
2. What does Ms. Goodman mean by the "stark contrast between reality and attitude"?
3. What is the significance of Anne Tyler's description of Pearl in her novel *Dinner at the Homesick Restaurant*?

"The American Myth of Failing Families." © 1982, The Boston Globe Newspaper Company/Washington Post Writers Group. Reprinted with permission.

I am glad I wasn't born in Muncie, Ind. Ever since Robert and Helen Lynd chose that city as a specimen of America in the 1920s, and dubbed it Middletown, the people of Muncie have had all the privacy of a community of laboratory rats.

At least three generations have spent their lives being observed, quantified, stashed away into some statistical pattern. Studies have been its most important product.

Now they are into a multi-media spring. They are being profiled individually in a public television series, *Middletown,* and profiled collectively in a book called "Middletown Families."

Middletown Message

Once again, the Muncie-Americans are bearing a message about our nation. A double message about the strength of our family life and the strength of our belief in its weakness.

On television I saw a portrait of the Snider family, headed by Howie Snider, ex-Marine, banjo-playing pizza parlor owner, one step ahead of his creditors. It was a tale full of the passionate intensity of family members.

Then in the book, I read a portrait of the whole city. After conducting 13 studies in the late 70s, an invasionary force of professors concluded that family life continues and in some ways is stronger than it was in the 1920s.

As sociologist Ted Caplow summarized, "We discovered increased family solidarity, a smaller generation gap, closer marital communication, more religion and less mobility."

The facts from Muncie were not shocking to those who have read other recent studies about American families. One after the other, researchers have checked in with news about the tenacity of family life. One after another, they have met head on with the conviction, even in Muncie, that families are falling apart.

How do we explain this stark contrast between reality and attitude? Is it because we confuse change with collapse? Is it because we see a half-empty glass?

Reality vs. Myth

There must be a slew of theories. In a recent piece, *Middletown* author Caplow even suggested that "the myth of the declining family" has some value for its believers. "When Middletown people compare their own families," he wrote, "with the 'average' or the 'typical' family, nearly all of them discover with pleasure that their own families are better than other people's."

But I don't agree that this myth developed as a subtle way to applaud our own superiority. I suspect that it has deeper, more complex roots.

I think that we all carry around inside us some primal scene of a family Eden, an ideal of family life. Among the strongest yearnings we take out of childhood is the desire to create this perfect family.

We share a longing to have or to be a perfect parent, perfect mate. We share a youthful certainty that we will be able to give and take perfect love. We will never be impatient, never yell at our children. They will never be distant or rude.

Families Are Healthier Than Ever

If Prof. Mary Jo Bane of Wellesley College is correct, we Americans for years have been singing a dirge over an institution that is neither dead nor dying but is in fact as healthy as it has ever been. . . .

The [much lamented] extended family never existed on a wide scale. Data from colonial America show that only 6 percent of U.S. households contained children, parents, and grandparents. . . .

More families have two parents now (84.3 per cent) than in colonial days (70 per cent).What divorce is doing to disrupt families today, death did in earlier times. As the death rate has dropped, the divorce rate has increased—but most divorced people remarry to stay.

It's doubtful that Americans move more often now than they did in the Nineteenth Century. So if mobility is fraying America's family and social fabric, it has been doing so for a long time.

There's no evidence that yesterday's mothers, laboring from dawn to dusk to do housework without labor-saving devices, devoted more time to their children than today's working mothers do.

August Gribbin, "The Family's Not 'Dying,'" *The National Observer*, 1977.

But each generation inevitably falls short of its own ideals about family life, and our personal disappointments harden into a national myth. I suspect that we date our belief in the decline of families from our eventual descent into reality. The vague sense that something is missing in our family becomes a general notion that something is missing in the family.

In Anne Tyler's moving novel, *Dinner at the Homesick Restaurant*, the elderly mother, Pearl, suddenly chokes up with a desire for the family life.

"Often like a child peering over the fence at somebody else's party, she gazes wistfully at other families and wonders what their secret is. They seem so close. It is that they're more religious? Or stricter, or more lenient? Could it be the fact that they participate in sports? Read books together? Have some common hobby? Recently she overheard a neighbor woman discussing her plans for Independence Day. Her family was having a picnic. Every member—child or grownup—was cooking his or her specialty. Those who were too little to cook were in charge of the paper plates.

"Pearl felt such a wave of longing that her knees went weak." She could be any of us.

119

How America's Families Are Changing

	1970	1982	Percent Change
Total US population	203,302,000	231,543,000	12%
Persons living alone	10,851,000	19,354,000	44
Married couples	44,728,000	50,294,000	11
Unmarried couples	523,000	1,863,000	72
Married couples with children	25,541,000	24,465,000	-4
Average size of household	3.3	2.72	-19
Children living with two parents	58,926,000	46,797,000	-21
Children living with one parent	8,230,000	13,701,000	40
Families with both husband and wife working	20,327,000	25,729,000*	21
Marriages performed	2,159,000	2,495,000	14
Divorces granted	708,000	1,180,000	40

*1981

Statistics from the US Department of Commerce and the US Bureau of Labor Statistics.

In real life there were, of course, ants at the picnic, and tears and tantrums. In real life, the neighbor occasionally also grew weak at the knees with her own longing for a perfect family.

So too in real life, our families fail our fantasies. We know that. But they aren't failures. At best, like the Sniders, they are complex, powerful, imperfect. And their strength is too easy to forget.

"*The challenge of the 80s will be to...create new family patterns based on equality and full human identity for both sexes.*"

The Family Needs to Be Changed

Betty Friedan

Betty Friedan, one of America's foremost spokeswomen for women's rights, is a writer, teacher, parent and activist for such issues as abortion reform, the Equal Rights Amendment, and reform in other areas of American life that affect women. Her most recent book, *The Second Stage* (1982), points out women's need for family as well as for personal identities acquired through careers outside the home. In the viewpoint below, Ms. Friedan discusses some of the ways she believes the family has to change to improve our society.

As you read, consider the following questions:
1. What statistics does Ms. Friedan quote to illustrate that the traditional family is changing?
2. According to the author, how does the United States differ from most advanced nations?
3. Why does Friedan feel that feminists should be supportive of the family?

Though the women's movement has changed all our lives, and our daughters take their own personhood and equality for granted, they—and we—are finding that it's not so easy to live with—or without—men and children—solely on the basis of that first feminist agenda. The great challenge we face in the 1980s is to frame a new agenda that makes it possible for women to be able to work and love in equality with men—and to choose, if they so desire, to have children.

For the choices we have sought in the '70s are not as simple as they once seemed. Indeed, some of the choices women are supposed to have won by now are not real choices at all. And even the measure of equality we have already achieved is not secure until we face these unanticipated conflicts between the demands of the workplace and professional success on the one hand, and demands of the family on the other. These conflicts seem insoluble because of the way the family and workplace have been structured in America.

Agenda for the '80s

The second feminist agenda, the agenda for the '80s, must call for the restructuring of home and work. But to confront the American family as it actually is today—instead of hysterically defending or attacking the family that is no more, "the classical family of Western nostalgia," as Stanford University sociologist William J. Goode calls it—means shattering an image that is still sacred to both church and state, to politicians on the right and left. And dispelling the mystique of the family may be even more threatening to some than unmasking the feminine mystique was a decade ago.

According to government statistics, only 17 percent of American households include a father who is the sole wage earner, a mother who is a full-time homemaker, and one or more children. (And one study found that one-third of all such full-time housewives planned to look for jobs.) There are more statistics on American households:
• 28 percent consist of both a father and a mother who are wage earners, with one or more children living at home.
• 32.4 percent consist of married couples with no children, or none living at home.
• 6.6 percent are headed by women who are single parents with one or more children at home.
• 0.7 percent are headed by men who are single parents with one or more children at home.

As Muriel Fox, president of NOW's Legal Defense and Education Fund, put it in her charge to the family assembly discussion leaders:

Our assembly will accept—rather than deny—the fact that 93 percent of American families today fit patterns other than the traditional one of a breadwinning father, a homemaking mother and two or more dependent children. We will accept the inevitability of continuing future change in the relationships and roles of men, women and children within families. And we will seek new responses to the conditions that are cause and effect of such change..."

In all, 43 percent of American wives with children under the age of 6 are working today, and by 1990, it is estimated that 64 percent will have jobs and only one out of three mothers, approximately, will be a full-time homemaker.

National Policy Needed

Yet the United States is one of the few advanced nations with no national policy of maternity and paternity leaves, no national policy encouraging flexible working arrangements and part-time and shared employment, and no national policy to provide child care for those who need it.

Confronting the crisis in child care, the family assembly is dispensing with rhetoric and theoretical arguments in favor of concrete proposals: new options, child-care solutions that have worked in other countries, child-care services that could be provided by a company or union in the actual workplace, home-based child care, commercial child-care services.

It seems clear to me that we will never bring about changes in the workplace, so necessary for the welfare of children and the family, if their only supporters and beneficiaries are women. The need for such innovations becomes urgent as more and more mothers enter the workplace, but they will come about only because more and more fathers demand them, too...

Concern about the Family

The truth is that if either sex has been in revolt against marriage, it is men, and that the male revolt against marriage started long before our own rebellion as feminists. . . .As feminists, we have always stood for men's as well as for women's liberation, which includes their right to be something other than husbands and breadwinners. . . .The problem, and it is a big one, is that men may have won their freedom before we win our battle against sexism. Women might like to be free-spirited adventurers too, but the female equivalent of "playboy" does not work well in a culture still riddled with misogyny. We still earn less than men, whether or not we have men to help support us. Which is only to say that the feminist agenda is as urgent as ever, and those who are concerned about "the family" should remember that we—and our sisters and daughters and mothers—are members of it also.

Barbara Ehrenreich, "The 'Playboy' Man and the American Family," *Ms.*, June 1983.

Why should women simply replace the glorification of domesticity with the glorification of work as their life and identity? Simply to reverse the roles of breadwinner and homemaker is no progress at all, not for women and not for men. The challenge of the 80s will be to transcend these polarities by creating new family patterns based on equality and full human identity for both sexes . . .

When extremists—both feminists and anti-feminists—perpetrate the myth that equality means death to the family, other women have a hard time figuring out what their real options are—and what their own real feelings are. But the underlying reality is no different for the most bitter feminists and most stridently fearful defenders of the family. None of us can depend throughout our new, long lives on that "family of Western nostalgia" to meet our needs for nurture and support, but all of us still have those needs. The answer is not to deny them, but to recognize and strengthen new family forms that can sustain us.

Importance of Family

To some it may sound strange for a feminist like myself to be arguing so passionately for the importance of families. Such arguments have been dismissed by some radical feminists as "reactionary family chauvinism." But it may very well be that the family, which has always been considered the bastion of conservatism, is already somehow being transformed by women's equality into a progressive political force. When men start assigning a higher priority to their families and self-fulfillment, and women a higher priority to independence and active participation in the "man's world," what happens to the supremacy of the corporate, bureaucratic system?

The new sharing of parental responsibilities and the envy many men are beginning to express of women's liberation suggest that the family, instead of being enemy territory to feminists, is really the underground through which secretly they reach into every man's life. The new urge of both women and men for meaning in their work and life, for love, roots and family—even though it may not resemble the ideal family that maybe never was—is a powerful force for change.

I'm not even altogether sure that the women's movement as such will be the main agent of this next stage of human liberation. But if we don't want to retreat, we must somehow turn this new corner toward the family of the future. Women must now confront anew their own needs for love and comfort and caring support, as well as the needs of children and men, for whom, I believe, we cannot escape bedrock human responsibility.

*"American business will pay an enormous price
if the traditional family should be smashed by
the militant feminists and their allies."*

Changing the Family
Would Be Disastrous

John Howard

John Howard is president of The Rockford Institute, "a non-
profit research center devoted to the study of the cultural
dynamics of a free society" located in Rockford, Illinois. In
the following viewpoint, Dr. Howard describes what he sees
as a significant threat to American business: feminist concepts
of a restructured family.

As you read, consider the following questions:
1. According to this viewpoint, what do feminists mean when
   they talk about "restructuring" the family?
2. Why does the writer believe this concept of restructuring is
   threatening to American business?
3. Does the writer seem to be concerned with the family itself
   or only with its effect on business?

From *Persuasion at Work* published by the Rockford Institute. Used by permission.

Trouble comes in bunches. It wasn't enough that the Ayatollah Khomeini and Soviet Russia both took action to shatter the most rudimentary elements of international relationships; a major campaign which challenges the basic relationships *within* the nation was also launched recently.

Two weeks after the Holy Man of the Shiite fanatics in Iran became the jailer of American embassy personnel, asserting that "America is the great Satan," the holy woman of the feminist fanatics, Betty Friedan, issued her manifesto which proclaimed that the traditional concepts of the family and of the workplace constitute another Satan, imposing evil and hardship on her constituency. On Sunday, November 18, 1979, the text of Ms. Friedan's proclamation was printed in the *New York Times*, the *Milwaukee Journal* and other papers across the country. This was but one element of a carefully orchestrated national campaign which had been begun on a massive scale when 33 women's magazines used their November issues to present a coordinated and intensive push for the Equal Rights Amendment.

What did she say? Well, it seems that women's lib has been too successful. She begins with vignettes of three career women who yearn for the satisfactions of a full family life. "It's hardly new," she observes, "for women to be concerned with the family. But aren't the women supposed to be liberating themselves from the family?" Yes and no is the answer to that one. "We are finding that it's not so easy to live with—or without—men and children . . . The choices we have sought in the 70s are not as simple as they once seemed." In order to have it both ways, Ms. Friedan announced that "the agenda of the 80s must call for the *restructuring of the institutions of home and work.*" (Emphasis added.)

"Restructuring"

That agenda may sound innocent enough, but "restructuring" does not mean mere alteration; it means providing full legal status as a family to any cluster of people that calls itself a family and revolutionizing the employer-employee relationships to accommodate the desires and whims of these clustered individuals. The actual implementation of her concept was made clear in the presentations and proposals of the New York City conference the next day. The 50-page program for the New York conference provides just one statement on the inside front cover. It set the stage for what is to follow, defining the family as "two or more persons who share resources, share responsibility for decisions, share values and goals, and have commitment to another over time. The family is that climate one 'comes home to' and it is this network of sharing and commitments that most accurately describes the family unit, *regardless of blood, legal ties, adoption, or marriage.*" (Emphasis added.) The business implications of this are staggering. Consider, for example, just the inhouse mechanics of maintaining the records on health care benefits if the law should be changed to recognize as a family any group that calls itself a family for any period of duration. On a much broader scale of concern, try to envision the probable level of personal stability and productivity of a future work force which, from childhood, has been reared and acculturated in a "home" environment where the group comprising the family has no legal or ethical responsibilities or permanence...

The feminist movement has won the day with its fight-for-your-rights-to-do-anything-you-please-and-reject-all-obligation philosophy that is now embraced throughout the opinion-making forces of the culture, if not in the minds and hearts of the people. This triumph must now be consolidated by laws which alter the structures of civilization so that women can have all the prerequisites of careerism and sexual profligacy without having to give birth to a baby if that is judged undesirable, or without sacrificing the joys of motherhood or being burdened with the inherent obligations of motherhood. The Equal Rights Amendment is seen as the legal vehicle which will assure all these conflicting wishes both in the home and in the place of work...

The Future Starts Here

The family, tied together with love, is the source of all productivity and growth. This is where it starts; this is where people gain their connections to the future, from which all these processes of saving and creativity derive.

George Gilder, "Family, Faith, and Economic Progress," *National Review*, April 15, 1983.

One cannot help wondering if all the 95 organizations listed in the program as official cosponsors of the New York conference had any advance notion of the nature and ideological orientation of the conference which they endorsed, or even if they do after the fact...

The juxtaposition of these titans of private enterprise with many movers and shakers of various radical causes in the joint advocacy of Betty Friedan's "agenda for the eighties" reenforces a point we have made repeatedly: The business community cannot afford to be ignorant of or indifferent to the major cultural and social issues of the day. The outcome of the *cultural* ferment that has been intensifying in the last decade and a half will have at least as great an impact on the viability of private enterprise as will the amount of oil available to us from foreign countries, or the character, judgment and priorities of the President and United States Congress.

Business Will Pay

American business will pay an enormous price if the traditional family should be smashed by the militant feminists and their allies who insist that our civilization must be "restructured" to meet all the diverse preferences and passions of individuals...

The philosophical basis of the NOW organization is well established and its concept of the family is scarcely one that anyone concerned about an ordered, stable and productive society would embrace. Generally, the business community has been alert and ingenious in meeting the challenges which fate, nature and human contrariness have presented. A new cultural challenge of vast proportions has surfaced. It calls for a response of an altogether different order and magnitude from anything that has been tried to date. Corporate naivete about the major social issues of the day is a critical flaw in its defense against the gathering forces of anticapitalism.

"MARRIED COUPLES SUING FOR RAPE, UNMARRIED COUPLES SUING FOR ALIMONY, THE DIVORCE RATE IS SOARING, ILLEGITIMATE BIRTHS ARE UP..... HONESTLY! SOMETIMES I WONDER WHATEVER BECAME OF THE NORMAL FAMILY UNIT, DEAR."

Jim Borgman, *Cincinnatti Enquirer*. Reprinted with permission.

Returning to where we began, the Iranian and Soviet assaults upon civilized standards of behavior, as awesome and perilous as they are, have at least been recognized by much of America, including the corporate community, as a peril that requires intelligent, coordinated and persistent counteraction. By contrast, the new campaign of militant feminism against the institutions of the marketplace and of the family (as it has been defined by religion, tradition, human experience and common sense) has elicited the concerted and overt *support* of many of the largest and most visible organizations that stand to lose the most if the campaign should succeed. Sobering, isn't it?

> "What's destroying the family isn't the family itself
> but the indifference of the rest of society."

The Family
Is Falling Apart

Susan Byrne and Urie Bronfenbrenner: An Interview

Susan Byrne, a freelance writer and former editor of *Psychology Today*, earned a Ph.D. in Anthropology from the University of California at Berkeley. She has written fiction as well as numerous articles on social science topics. Urie Bronfenbrenner, noted Professor of Psychology at Cornell University, was born in Moscow but grew up and was educated in the United States. He received his Ph.D. from the University of Michigan. The author of several volumes on human development, Dr. Bronfenbrenner has studied family life in Europe, Asia, and North America. In the following viewpoint, Dr. Byrne questions Dr. Bronfenbrenner about his concerns for the American family.

As you read, consider the following questions:
1. In what sense does Dr. Bronfenbrenner believe the family is "falling apart"? What does he think is causing this?
2. What does he think should be done to strengthen the family?
3. What does he see as the positive values of the family?

Reprinted from *Psychology Today Magazine.* Copyright © 1977, American Psychological Association

Susan Byrne: You've been studying the family for years. What is happening to America's families?

Urie Bronfenbrenner: The family is falling apart. There is a lot of evidence to substantiate this. Since World War II the extended family of several generations, with all its relatives, has practically disappeared in this country. Even the small nuclear family of mother, father, and the kids is in decline.

Today, more than one-sixth of all children in our country are living in single-parent families. The single parent is usually a woman, the head of an independent family, and she almost always works full time. Meanwhile, despite birth control, the number of unwed mothers is skyrocketing.

All these developments have left many children without any care at all.

Byrne: So we have a great many families consisting of women and children—with fathers possibly on the periphery.

Bronfenbrenner: Exactly. And there has been a rapid rise in the number of mothers who work. Over 50 percent of women with school-aged children are now employed. So are over one-third of those with children under six. In fact, one-third of women with children under three are working. We've got a situation in which the father is working and the mother is working, too.

Empty Houses

Byrne: Which means that they are not at home much of the time.

Bronfenbrenner: That's right, and the question is, who *is* caring for America's children? The answer is disturbing. Fewer and fewer parents are doing their job of caring for children. Meanwhile, substitute-care facilities are in very low supply, at least in this country. They're expensive for those who can afford them and practically nonexistent for those who can't. Just this past year, we've again seen a day-care bill vetoed. The U.S. is now the only developed country in the world that doesn't have a national program providing child care for working parents, minimum family income and health care for families with young children.

Increasing numbers of children are coming home to empty houses. If there's any reliable predictor of trouble, it probably begins with children coming home to an empty house, whether the problem is reading difficulties, truancy, dropping out, drug addiction, or childhood depression.

Byrne: An empty house—a poignant symbol of nobody caring.

Bronfenbrenner: And so simple. I'm not talking about the lack of some fancy developmental treatment or intensive care for kids; I'm talking about empty, about the lack of *any* care.

Sometimes children are alone for hours with nothing but television. The TV isn't going to care for them. What happens? The kids find other kids who are coming home to empty houses. They create a peer-group culture, and it's likely to be an ugly culture—a culture of destroy, of break, of act out. The essence of it is *anomie*, a social and emotional disintegration, inside and outside. Frightening as it may be, this screaming for help isn't occurring just among a small minority of children. Hardly a school in the country doesn't have a problem with vandalism and violence. Think what that suggests. A major institution, charged with preparing the next generation for adult life, is a focus of aimless destruction.

Bryne: Before we talk about schools, tell me why you see the family falling apart. What's causing it?

Bronfenbrenner: Well, first of all, it's not because parents are irresponsible or children are intractable—although children having received inadequate care are more difficult these days. What's destroying the family isn't the family itself but the indifference of the rest of society. The family takes a low priority.

Byrne: Perhaps we feel it's more important to follow our own personal stars than to preserve the family.

Bronfenbrenner: That's right. Move the old folks to Florida so they can live their life and we can live ours. It's all very understandable. This whole way of life is fine if you're young, sexy, and full of verve. But if you happen to be a child, or sick, or lonely, or old- -and all of us are at some time—you need somebody else. If that somebody else is doing his own thing, he's not there.

Byrne: We're coming to expect the government to take care of dependent people in America. What's happening in other countries? Are they having the same problems?

Bronfenbrenner: Yes, but many of them are doing more about them. They are counteracting the breakdown by providing support systems. America isn't alone in wanting the government to take care of people in trouble. Other countries do the same—better than we do sometimes. But many countries also build around the family.

Byrne: Are you saying we don't have those traditions other counties do?

Bronfenbrenner: They don't seem as strong. We're a young rambunctious society, only 200 years old, and we don't have very much of that glue, whatever it is, that can preserve a society's solidarity while we rush to the moon and back. Our social fabric is beginning to rip.

Jobs and Neighborhoods

Byrne: How do we mend it?

Bronfenbrenner: I think the two most powerful settings that affect the family, and thus the next generation, are the world of business—work and jobs—and the world of the neighborhood—the people around us, where we live and our children grow up. I believe that if we could make certain changes in these institutions we'd have better child care, happier families, and a more caring society generally. And I mean real changes.

As for work, we're finally beginning to come to our senses in recognizing that the larger half of our population, women, have talents and abilities. Women are going to work, and they deserve to do so. Yet we keep the old male work rules, nine to five, 40 hours a week, and if there's overtime you do it or you don't keep your job.

Neither men nor women can combine working and parenting under those rules. We need new ways of working.

As for the neighborhood, it can provide an informal support system for the family but it usually doesn't. Here's a small example: if a parent has to go some place, it's nice to be able to take the child next door for substitute care, or have a neighbor come in. Well, that's the highly efficient old way. Now it has to be on a paying basis.

Byrne: People who have never juggled children and careers may have no idea of what it takes to commute between child-care facilities and work, of the waste of time and energy you could spend on the children and at work.

Endangered Family

The family is the fundamental building block and the basic unit of our society, and its continued health is a prerequisite for a healthy and prosperous nation. . . .

There is a vicious assault on the American family. More television programs depict homes of divorced or of single parents than depict the traditional family. Nearly every major family-theme TV program openly justifies divorce, homosexuality, and adultery. Some sociologiests believe that the family unit, as we know it, could disappear by the year 2000. Increased divorce and remarriage have broken family loyalty, unity, and communications.

Jerry Falwell, *Listen, America!* 1980.

Bronfenbrenner: You've put your finger on the point. It's a terrible waste of time and energy. You can be a devoted, loving parent but be so hassled by this transportation business that you can't function effectively. The great American profession for married, middle-class females is chauffeur. It's not a profession they choose, but one they are forced into. In many neighborhoods zoning laws do not permit day-care centers to exist legally.

Byrne: Suppose there were decent day-care centers located near people's homes and jobs. Does day care have an adverse effect on a child's development? Might it be bad for a child emotionally, socially, or intellectually?

Bronfenbrenner: As far as I know—and I've reviewed the evidence on this question—there is no appreciable difference between day care and home care provided two conditions are met. First, it must be good quality care and much of ours isn't, since we are not willing to pay for it. Second, and equally important, the child should spend a substantial amount of time with somebody who's crazy about him . . .

132

But it is also good to be with people who are not crazy about him. He needs both kinds of experience. He needs some mothering, some fathering, some day care, even some coolness toward him. But all of these needs must be met. Our country's problem is that we're not meeting these needs properly. Increasingly we're not caring for children at all.

That is why I want to see changes in the world of work, so that both parents can work parttime on a flexible schedule.

Many people consider child rearing a low-status activity. That should not be the reason for instituting day care . . .

Social Policy

We have to give at least as much attention to social policy as we give to material technology. We wouldn't think, for example, of rocketing a man into space without drawing the blueprints first, testing the components one by one, and finally sending the rocket up without anybody in it to make sure people won't get hurt. But look at what we do with social vehicles. No pretesting, no trying out the parts, nothing. Just send it out there with people in it. And people get hurt, especially women and children. The welfare system is a case in point.

Of course, once we do apply our best minds to the problem of caring for children, I think we'll have the deflating experience of rediscovering the wheel. We'll find that families, after all, are really very efficient.

Byrne: They did evolve specifically to nurture the young.

Bronfenbrenner: Yes, and that is why we don't need a new social vehicle. All we have to do is to create new conditions to enable families to do what they do better than anybody else. We need to make it possible for children and adults to enter each other's worlds. It will be good for both of them.

Double Doses

With new and old patterns both in the air, it is all too human for each partner to reach out for the double dose of privileges, those of the old and those of the new role, leaving to the mate the double dose of obligation.

Mirra Komarovksy, *Women in the Modern World,* 1953.

Byrne: People tend to forget these days that the family is a benefit for adults, too. The family may be our last sanctuary in an increasingly complicated and maybe frustrating world.

Bronfenbrenner: Yes, but the family is more than that, less sad than that. The family is also the first sanctuary. If a person gets a good start in the family, he can cope with all sorts of problems in later life. In that primitive Ping-Pong game, that back-and-forth between an infant and its caretaker, a person learns how to get his basic needs satisfied by other human beings. As adults we're not conscious of using

133

these skills in our relationships with our colleagues and friends, but we do.

In a sense, the family is with us always. And it is an exciting, and rewarding venture.

Byrne: The family can be the villain, too, can't it?

Bronfenbrenner: Look, even in the best of times the family obviously can have problems. But does family life typically hurt people as badly as no care at all? That's the issue . . .

The relationships in families are the juice of life, the longings and frustrations and intense loyalties. We get our strength from those relationships, we enjoy them, even the painful ones. Of course, we also get some of our problems from them, but the power to survive those problems comes from the family, too. I only wish we could examine today's family without nostalgia. We could learn something about its great strengths and its terrible weaknesses and could see our task more clearly.

If we'd pay as much attention to families as we pay to firearms and football, this country would be a lot healthier and happier.

"Not only is the family alive and well,
it is aliver and weller."

The Family
Is Alive and Well

U.S. News & World Report

In their June 16, 1980 issue, *U.S. News & World Report* ran a special section on "the American family." It included an analysis of how families are changing and close looks at seven kinds of families. The following viewpoint, taken from the first article in the special section, expresses the belief that American families remain strong although they change.

As you read, consider the following questions:
1. Why do you think Mary Margaret Carr says "It's dangerous . . . to say that the only strong family is one that meets my narrow concept or your narrow concept"?
2. According to the writer, what are some of the changes coming about that will continue to strengthen the family?
3. Why does the writer think that people will want to keep a strong concept of family?

"The American Family: Bent—But Not Broken." From a copyrighted article in *U.S. News & World Report*, June 16, 1980.

Challenged and buffeted as rarely before, the American family once again is changing to survive in a changing world.

The latest accommodations—heartening to some, while alarming to others—underscore the resilience of an institution that has repeatedly withstood predictions of an early demise.

Mankind's most basic and oldest social unit, the family, has "taken many forms over history and conformed to the social forces of that era," observes John P. Vincent, associate professor of psychology at the University of Houston. "We're seeing a natural evolution now."

Cries of crisis, Vincent says, only document the family's "growing pains."

Sacred, mysterious and sometimes misunderstood, the family today is assuming a variety of forms, each reflecting an adjustment to the revolutionary social changes that have swept the nation in the past generation. Few realize just how far-reaching the adaptations have been.

The "traditional" American family, for example, still portrayed by advertising, children's literature and popular movies now is in a minority. A scant 13 percent of the nation's families include a working father, stay-at-home mother and one or more children.

Defining "Family"

Today, the definitions of family are as varied and pragmatic as the nation itself. "It's dangerous," notes Mary Margaret Carr, executive director of the Children's Service and Family Counseling Center in Atlanta, "to say that the only strong family is one that meets my narrow concept or your narrow concept."

Behind the changes lie new economic conditions and widening horizons for women. More than half the nation's mothers work outside the home. Six out of 10 married women with school-age children work. Of married women with children under 6 years old, 43 percent work.

Millions of preschool children now are cared for in day-care centers—a development that still sparks controversy. One expert estimates that 64 percent of all children between the ages of 3 and 5 spend part of their day in facilities outside their home.

Says Alfred J. Kahn of the Columbia School of Social Work: "All the research we have suggests that it doesn't do anything to a child. They grow up like everybody else."

Traditionalists insist, however, that it may take years for the long-term effects of such care to become clear.

Contributing to the use of day-care facilities is the growing number of children who live with single parents. Eighteen million children live in what once were called "broken homes" before divorce became so rampant that one marriage ends for every two that begin. According to one Census Bureau expert, fully 45 percent of the children born in 1978 may spend at least part of their childhoods with only one parent.

Still another milestone of change is the birth of the two-career marriage—a partnership that pays off financially. The more than 19 million families that had at least two wage earners in 1979 made an average of $509 a week—more than $26,000 a year—compared with $305 a week for families with single breadwinners.

Economic hardship accounts for the number of mature children returning home after college. "I couldn't afford to live away from home," says Michele Duwelius of Des Moines, who graduated last year from Iowa State University.

The "refilled nest," cautions Drake University sociologist Lewis McNurlen, is not always a happy home, noting: "The tension can get much deeper than questions about whether mom still picks up the towels."

Adds one couple whose children came home: "We ate what we wanted when we wanted. We enjoyed these new freedoms, and then suddenly somebody came home with an appetite."

The proliferation of family forms underscores their adaptability. "The family is not in a state of disrepair," says Bertram Cohler of the University of Chicago. "Not only is the family alive and well, it is aliver and weller."

So sweeping are the changes that many living arrangements once considered immoral, if not illegal, now are accepted as "families." More than 2.7 million men and women live together unmarried, buying and selling houses and even raising the children of one or both partners' previous marriages. Homosexuals openly share households and take marriage vows. Communal living is enjoying acceptance.

The law, too, is changing to match such sweeping social developments. Live-in companions now qualify for "palimony." Moreover, courts are awarding alimony to husbands as well as wives, contending that to bar such payments to men is sex discrimination . . . .

What Lies Ahead?

What lies ahead for the American family? The willingness to innovate and adapt clearly highlights widespread yearning for the benefits of family. Interest in it is flourishing. Millions watch television programs such as "All in the Family" and "One Day at a Time" that detail changing patterns of family life . . . .

Government and industry are beginning to face pressure to accommodate the changes in the family. Congress is at work on the tax code to reverse a penalty on married couples. Social Security laws soon may change to more equitably compensate women who stay at home to raise children.

Workers are negotiating for workplace day-care centers, flexible hours and even paternity leave to help ease the burden of family responsibilities.

Businesses in one Chicago suburb can turn to the Niles Family Service to get guidance on helping workers with family problems. "The program is an early-detection program," says psychologist Ronald

Martin. "I train supervisors not to become amateur psychologists, but to document declining work performance" so that professional help can be brought in.

Still, authorities contend that much needs to be done. A recent study by a pair of specialists at the Columbia School of Social Work warns that efforts by government to advance the interests of families are "unlikely to yield much or even be launched unless there is greater determination expressed outside the government that family well-being be guarded in the course of general policymaking."

Yet families hunger for action. A Gallup Poll conducted for the White House Conference on Families [1980] found that 61 percent of families polled considered their family the most important element in their lives, but nearly half said family life had gotten worse.

A Return to Normal

Despite their concerns about divorce rates and unwed mothers, most students of American house and home seem fairly optimistic. Harvard's [George] Masnick argues that what appeared to be sweeping changes during the 1970s are actually a return to something more like normal. It was the 1950s and 1960s, with their earlier and higher rate of marriages and their extraordinary birthrates, that were unusual. "We must be careful not to assume that just because the older generation came first, their family patterns were more typical of 20th century American family life," writes [sociologist Andrew] Cherlin of Johns Hopkins. "A close look at the historical record suggests that in some ways, the 1970s were most consistent with the longterm trends in family life."

"Death of the Family," *Newsweek*, January 17, 1983.

And George Masnick and Mary Jo Bane of the Joint Center for Urban Studies of the Massachusetts Institute of Technology and Harvard University report in *The Nation's Families:1960-1990* that society needs to adjust to fewer married couples, more unattached individuals and the growing variety of family relationships that Americans encounter through life.

Reason for optimism exists, however. "We're a little behind most of the world because America tends to be afraid to tamper with the family," notes Columbia's Kahn. "But it's going to discover that since families are precious and children are precious, it's going to have to do something about it so that children can be reared and adults can work."

Change for the Better

While the years of transition may be difficult, many observers foresee both society and the family emerging better prepared to deal with the 1980s.

As Masnick and Bane conclude in their recent study, "We expect changes in households and families to be accompanied by new relationships within families and among households, the community, the economy and the government."

Indeed, the American family may be different—but it is far from dead. As one specialist puts it: "I think people will think the family unit is an important one to maintain. It has something to do with their identity, practical reasons like support systems, and it can provide a richness to life."

Understanding Words in Context

Readers occasionally come across words which they do not recognize. And frequently, because the reader does not know a word or words, he or she will not fully understand the passage being read. Obviously, the reader can look up an unfamiliar word in a dictionary. However, by carefully examining the word in the context in which it is used, the word's meaning can often be determined. A careful reader may find clues to the meaning of the word in surrounding words, ideas and attitudes.

The excerpts below come primarily from the viewpoints in this chapter. In each excerpt, a word is printed in italics. Try to determine the meaning of each word by reading the excerpt. Under each excerpt you will find four definitions for the italicized word. Choose the one that is closest to your understanding of the word.

Finally, use a dictionary to see how well you have understood the words in context. It will be helpful to discuss with others the clues which helped you decide each word's meaning.

1. But each generation *INEVITABLY* falls short of its own ideals about family life and our personal disappointments harden into a national myth.

   INEVITABLY means
   a) oddly
   c) sometimes
   b) unavoidably
   d) never

2. Often, like a child peering over the fence at somebody else's party, she gazes *WISTFULLY* at other families and wonders what their secret is.

   WISTFULLY means
   a) angrily
   c) longingly
   b) curiously
   d) fearfully

3. In seeking to "defend" the family they strike out at anybody who *DIVERGES* from what they consider good and "decent" and right.

   DIVERGES means
   a) comes from   b) is militant about
   c) separates or moves away from   d) suffers or accepts

4. But it may very well be that the family, which has always been considered the *BASTION* of conservatism, is already somehow being transformed by women's equality into a progressive political force.

   BASTION means
   a) enemy   b) child
   c) fortress   d) beneficiary

5. The *JUXTAPOSITION* of these titans of private enterprise with many movers and shakers of various radical causes. . . reenforces a point we have made repeatedly: The business community cannot afford to be ignorant of or indifferent to the major cultural and social issues of the day.

   JUXTAPOSITION means
   a) putting at opposite extremes   b) placement side by side
   c) working against each other   d) making great profit from

6. So we have a great many families consisting of women and children—with fathers possibly on the *PERIPHERY*.

   PERIPHERY means
   a) outside   b) inside
   c) center   d) run

7. Families are not falling apart only because parents are irresponsible or children are *INTRACTABLE*.

   INTRACTABLE means
   a) irresponsible   b) responsible
   c) not loved   d) difficult to manage

8. Nor can the Virginia Slims poll. . .help but further *POLARIZE* Americans' attitudes toward the family. Women, and many men, find themselves lining up as if in battle lines.

   POLARIZE means
   a) separate into extremely   b) unify into a strong whole
       different views   d) weaken
   c) change into new forms

Bibliography

The following list of periodical articles deals with the subject matter of this chapter.

Mary Catherine Bateson "Caring for Children, Caring for the Earth," *Christianity & Crisis*, March 31, 1980.

Anthony Brandt "Father Love," *Esquire*, November 1982.

Dr. T. Barry Brazleton, interviewed "The Secret to Raising Healthy, Happy Children,"*U.S. News & World Report*, December 14, 1981.

Ruth Clark & Greg Martire "Americans Still in a Family Way," *Public Opinion*, October/November 1979.

Mario O. Cuomo "The Family: The Basic Unit of Civilization," *Vital Speeches of the Day*, February 15, 1980.

Michael D'Innocenzo "The Family Under Fire: Strategies for Coping," *Vital Speeches of the Day*, May 1, 1977.

Jean Beth Elshtain "Family Reconstruction," *Commonweal*, August 1, 1980.

James L. Framo "The Friendly Divorce," *Psychology Today*, February 1978.

Linda Bird Franke & Others "The Children of Divorce," *Newsweek*, February 11, 1980.

Nathan Glazer "The Rediscovery of the Family," *Commentary*, March 1978.

Andrew Hacker "Farewell to the Family?" *New York Review of Books*, March 18, 1982.

Stanley Hauerwas "The Moral Meaning of the Family," *Commonweal*, August 1980.

Wally Helgeson "Theoretical Families," *Harper's*, January 1982.

Lee Hollard "The Crisis of Family," *Sojourners*, May 1982.

John A. Howard "The Contra-Family Forces in the Culture," *Vital Speeches of the Day*, October 1978.

Jonathan Kellerman "My Turn: Big Brother and Big Mother," *Newsweek*, January 12, 1981.

Arthur Kornhaber "On the Eve of Grandparents Day, a Psychiatrist Pleads for a Reunion of the American Family," *People*, September 14, 1981.

Peter C. Kratcoski "The American Family: Decline or Rebirth," *USA Today*, September 1982.

Madeline Lee "At Holiday Time—Can Friends Be Family?" *Ms.*, December 1981.

Onalee McGraw	"Recovery of the American Family Nothing Less than Recovery of Our Common Humanity," *Conservative Digest*, March 1981.
Margaret Mead	"Can the American Family Survive?" *Redbook*, February 1977.
Daniel Patrick Moynihan	"Rescuing the Family," *America*, July 26, 1980.
Ms.	"Who Is the Real American Family?" August 1978.
Newsweek	"Death of the Family?" January 17, 1983.
Maya Pines interviews Jay Haley	"Restoring Law and Order to the Family," *Psychology Today*, November 1982.
Barbara Katz Rothman	"How Science Is Redefining Parenthood," *Ms.* July/August 1982.
Diane Ravitch	"In the Family's Way," *The New Republic*, June 28, 1980.
Laurence Shames	"Wolves Mate for Life," *Esquire*, November 1982.
Jagna Wojcicka Sharff	"Free Enterprise and the Ghetto Family," *Psychology Today*, March 1981.
J. Francis Stafford	"An Agenda for a National Family Policy," *America*, June 14, 1980.
J. Francis Stafford	"American Families and Federal Policy," *America*, December 25, 1982.
Catherine R. Stimpson	"The Company of Children," *Ms.*, July/August 1982.
U.S. News & World Report	Special section on "The American Family," June 16, 1980.
Judith S. Wallerstein & Joan B. Kelly	"California's Children of Divorce," *Psychology Today*, January 1980.
Marie Winn	"The Loss of Childhood," *New York Times Magazine*, May 8, 1983.

Bibliography of Books

Carol Adams
& Rae Laurikietis

The Gender Trap: A Closer Look at Sex Roles, 3 Vols. Revised for American readers by Jill Dunnell Sellers. Virago, Ltd., 1977.

Daniel Amneus

Back to Patriarchy. New Rochelle, NY: Arlington House Publishers, 1979.

Helen Andelin

Fascinating Womanhood. Santa Barbara, CA: Pacific Press, 1972.

Burt Avedon

Ah, Men: What Do Men Want? A Panorama of the Male in Crisis—His Past Problems, Present Uncertainties, Future Goals. New York: A & W Publishers, Inc., 1980.

Mary Jo Bane

Here to Stay: American Families in the Twentieth Century. New York: Basic Books, 1978.

Grace Baruch & Others

Lifeprints: New Patterns of Love & Work for Today's Women. New York: McGraw-Hill, 1983.

Karl Bednark

The Male in Crisis. New York: McGraw-Hill, 1983.

William R. Beer

Househusbands: Men and Housework in American Families. New York: J.F. Bergin/Praeger, 1983.

Brigette Berger
& Peter L. Berger

The War Over the Family: Capturing the Middle Ground. New York: Anchor Books/Doubleday, 1983.

Eugene C. Bianchi &
Rosemary Radford
Ruether

From Machismo to Mutuality: Woman-Man Liberation. New York: Paulist Press, 1976.

Caroline Bird

Born Female. New York: Pocket Books, 1968.

Robert Brannon &
Deborah David, Editors

The Forty-Nine Percent Majority: The Male Sex Role. Reading, MA: Addison-Wesley, 1976.

Myron Brenton

The American Male. Greenwich, CT: Fawcett Publications, 1966.

Theodore Caplow
& Others

Middletown Families: Fifty Years of Change & Continuity. Minneapolis: University of Minnesota Press, 1982.

William H. Chafe

Women and Equality: Changing Patterns in American Culture. New York: Oxford University Press, 1977.

William H. Chafe	*The American Woman: Her Changing Social, Economic and Political Roles.* New York: Oxford University Press, 1977.
Janet Saltzman Chafetz	*Masculine/Feminine or Human? An Overview of the Sociology of Gender Roles*, 2nd Edition. Itasca, IL: F.E. Peacock Publishers, Inc., 1978.
Phyllis Chesler & Emily Jane Goodman	*Women, Money & Power.* New York: William Morrow & Company, Inc., 1976.
Chris Cook, Editor	*The Men's Survival Resource Book: On Being a Man in Today's World.* Minneapolis: M.S.R.B. Press, 1978.
Joan M. & Larry L. Constantine	*Group Marriage: A Study of Contemporary Multilateral Marriage.* New York: Macmillan, 1973.
Karen DeCrow	*Sexist Justice.* New York: Vintage Books, 1974.
Midge Dector	*The New Chastity and Other Arguments Against Women's Liberation.* New York: Coward, McCann & Geoghegan, Inc., 1972.
Carl N. Degler	*At Odds: Women and the Family in America from the Revolution to the Present.* New York: Oxford University Press, 1980.
Peter DeJong & Donald R. Wilson	*Husband & Wife: The Sexes in Scripture & Society.* Grand Rapids, MI: Zondervan Publishing House, 1979.
Collette Dowling	*The Cinderella Complex: Women's Hidden Fear of Independence.* New York: Pocket Books, 1981.
Editorial Research Reports	*The Changing American Family.* Washington, DC: Congressional Quarterly, Inc., 1979.
Editorial Research Reports	*The Women's Movement: Achievements and Effects.* Washington, DC: Congressional Quarterly, Inc., 1977.
Barbara Ehrenreich	*The Hearts of Men; American Dreams and the Flight from Commitment.* New York: Anchor/Doubleday, 1983.
Jerry Falwell	*Listen, America!* New York: Bantam, 1980.
Warren Farrell	*The Liberated Man.* New York: Bantam, 1975.
Marc Feigen Fasteau	*The Male Machine.* New York: Delta/Dell Publishing Co., Inc., 1975.
Bruce Feirstein	*Real Men Don't Eat Quiche.* New York: Pocket Books, 1981.

Carol Felsenthal	*Phyllis Schlafly, The Sweetheart of the Moral Majority*. Chicago: Regnery Gateway, 1982.
Peter Filene	*Him/Herself: Sex Roles in Modern America*. New York: Harcourt, Brace, Jovanovich, 1975.
Anne Bowen Follis	*"I'm Not a Women's Libber, But. . ."* New York: Avon, 1982.
Jim & Andrea Fordham	*The Assault on the Sexes*. New Rochelle, New York: Arlington House, Publishers, 1977.
Suzanne Fremon, Editor	*Women and Men: Tradition and Trends*. New York: The Reference Shelf/The H.W. Wilson Company, 1977.
Betty Friedan	*The Second Stage*. New York: Summit Books, 1981.
General Mills	*The General Mills Reports on Families*, General Mills, Inc., P.O. Box 1113, Minneapolis, MN 55440.
Diane Gersoni-Stavn	*Sexism and Youth*. New York: R.R. Bowker Company, 1979.
Mark Gerzon	*A Choice of Heroes: The Changing Faces of American Manhood*. New York: Houghton-Mifflin, 1982.
George F. Gilder	*On Wealth and Poverty*. New York: Basic Books, Inc., Publishers, 1981.
Natalie Gittelson	*Dominus: A Woman Looks at Men's Lives*. New York: Farrar, Straus, and Giroux, 1978.
Erving Goffman	*Gender Advertisements*. New York: Harper & Row, 1979.
Herb Goldberg	*The New Male-Female Relationship*. New York: Morrow, 1983.
John Gordon	*The Myth of the Monstrous Male—and Other Feminist Fables*. Chicago: Playboy Press, 1982.
Adolph Güggenbuhl-Craig	*Marriage: Dead or Alive*. Dallas, TX: Spring Publications, 1977.
Max Gunther	*Virility 8: A Celebration of the American Male*. Chicago: Playboy Press, 1975.
Richard Hagen	*The Bio-Sexual Factor*. Garden City, NY: Doubleday & Company, Inc., 1979.
Harold H. Hart, Editor	*Marriage: For and Against*. New York: Hart Publishing Company, Inc., 1972.
Carolyn G. Heilbrun	*Reinventing Womanhood*. New York: W.W. Norton & Company, 1979.

Terry Hekker

Ever Since Adam & Eve: The Satisfactions of Housewifery and Motherhood in the Age·of Do-Your-Own-Thing. New York: William Morrow and Company, Inc., 1979.

Janet M. Hooks

Women's Occupations through Seven Decades, Women's Bureau Bulletin #218. Washington, DC: U.S. Department of Labor, 1976.

Jane Howard

Families. New York: Simon & Schuster, 1978.

Elizabeth Janeway

Man's World, Woman's Place: A Study in Social Mythology. New York: Morrow, 1971.

O.R. Johnson

Who Needs the Family? Downers Grove, IL: Inter-Varsity Press, 1980.

Robert A. Johnson

He: Understanding Masculine Psychology. New York: Harper & Row, 1977.

Leo Kanowitz

Equal Rights: The Male Stake. Albuquerque: The University of New Mexico Press, 1981.

Alexandra Kaplan & Joan P. Bean, Editors

Beyond Sex-Role Stereotypes: Readings Toward a Psychology of Androgeny. Boston: Little, Brown & Company, 1976.

Harvey E. Kaye

Male Survival: Masculinity without Myth. New York: Grosset & Dunlap Publishers, 1974.

Mirra Komarovsky

Dilemmas of Masculinity. New York: W.W. Norton and Co., 1976.

Michael Korda

Male Chauvinism: How It Works. New York: Random House, 1973.

Rita Kramer

In Defense of the Family: Raising Children in America Today. New York: Basic Books, 1983.

Tim LaHaye

Understanding the Male Temperament: What Every Man Would Like to Tell His Wife about Himself...But Won't. Old Tappan, NJ: Power Books/Fleming H. Revell Company, 1977.

Judith Long Laws

The Second X: Sex Role and Social Role. New York: Elsevier, 1979.

William J. Lederer

Marital Choices: Forecasting, Assessing, & Improving a Relationship. New York: W.W. Norton & Co., 1981.

Gerda Lerner

The Female Experience: An American Documentary. Indianapolis: The Bobbs-Merrill Company, Inc., 1977.

Gerda Lerner

The Woman in American History. Menlo Park, CA: Addison-Wesley Publishing Co., 1971.

Daniel J. Levinson

The Seasons of a Man's Life. New York: Alfred A. Knopf, Inc., 1978.

Sar A. Levitan & Richard
S. Belous

What's Happening to the American Family?
Baltimore: The Johns Hopkins University
Press, 1981.

Robert A. Lewis,
Editor

Men in Difficult Times: Masculinity Today and
Tomorrow. Englewood Cliffs, NJ: Prentice
Hall, 1980.

Karen Lindsay

Friends as Family: New Kinds of Families and
What They Could Mean to You. Boston:
Beacon, 1981.

Robert H. Loeb

Breaking the Sex Role Barrier. New York:
Franklin Watts, 1977.

Margaret Mead

Male and Female: A Study of the Sexes in a
Changing World. New York: William Morrow
and Company, 1949.

Wendy McElroy, Editor

Freedom, Feminism, and the State: An Overview
of Individualist Feminism. CATO Institute, 224
Second Street, S.E., Washington, D.C. 20003,
1982.

Virginia Ramey
Mollenkott

Women, Men, and the Bible. Nashville, TN:
Abingdon, 1977.

John Money &
Anke A. Ehrhardt

Sexual Signatures: On Being a Man or a
Woman. Boston: Little, Brown & Company,
1975.

Ashley Montagu

On the Natural Superiority of Women. New
York: Macmillan Publishing Co., Inc., 1968.

Marabel Morgan

The Total Woman. Old Tappan, NJ: F.H.
Revell, 1973.

Robin Morgan

The Anatomy of Freedom: Feminism, Physics,
& Global Politics. New York: Doubleday/An-
chor, 1982.

Pierre Mornell

Passive Men, Wild Women. New York: Simon
& Schuster, 1979.

Kathleen Newland

The Sisterhood of Man. New York: W.W. Norton & Co., 1979.

Jack Nichols

Men's Liberation: A New Definition of
Masculinity. New York: Penguin Books, 1975.

Ann Oakley

Subject Woman. New York: Pantheon Books,
1981.

Tillie Olson

Silences. New York: Delta/Dell Publishing
House, 1978.

Joseph H. Pleck

The Myth of Masculinity. Cambridge, MA:
M.I.T. Press, 1981.

Joseph H. Pleck &
Jack Sawyer, Editors

Men and Masculinity. Englewood Cliffs, NJ:
Prentice-Hall, Inc., 1974.

Lettie C. Pogrebin	*Growing Up Free: A Guide to Non-Sexist Child Rearing.* New York: McGraw-Hill, 1980.
Willie Mae Reid	*Black Women's Struggle for Equality.* New York: Pathfinder Press, 1976.
Ira L. Reiss	*The Family System in America.* New York: Holt, Rinehart & Winston, 1980.
Caryl Rivers, Rosalind Burnett, & Grace Baruch	*Beyond Sugar and Spice: How Women Grow, Learn, & Thrive.* New York: G.P. Putnam's Sons, 1979.
Joanne Bunker Rohrbaugh	*Women: Psychology's Puzzle.* New York: Basic Books, 1979.
Roper Organization, Inc.	*The Virginia Slims American Women's Polls.* Philip Morris, U.S.A., 120 Park Avenue, New York, NY 10017.
Susan C. Ross	*The Rights of Women.* New York: American Civil Liberties Union.
David Sammons	*The Marriage Option: Why It Remains the Best Alternative.* Boston: Beacon Press, 1977.
Peggy Reeves Sanday	*Female Power & Male Dominance: On the Origin of Sexual Inequality.* London: Cambridge University Press, 1981.
Alice C. Sargent	*Beyond Sex Roles.* St. Paul: West Publishing Company, 1977.
Donald M. Scott & Bernard Wishy	*America's Families: A Documentary History.* New York: Harper & Row, 1982.
Patricia Sexton	*The Feminized Male.* New York: Vintage Books, 1969.
Evelyn Shapiro & Barry M. Shapiro	*The Women Say/The Men Say: Women's Liberation and Men's Consciousness.* New York: Delta/Dell Publishing Co., 1979.
Jacqueline Simenauer & David Carroll	*Singles: The New Americans.* New York: Simon and Schuster, 1982.
Philip Slater	*Footholds: Understanding the Shifting Sexual and Family Tensions in Our Culture.* Boston: Beacon Press, 1977.
Kenneth G. & Floy M. Smith	*Learning to Be a Woman.* Madison, WI: Inter-Varsity Christian Fellowship of the United States of America, 1980.
Kenneth G. & Floy M. Smith	*Learning to Be a Man.* Madison, WI: Inter-Varsity Christian Fellowship of the United States of America, 1980.
Jon Snodgrass	*For Men Against Sexism: A Book of Readings.* Albion, CA: Times Change Press, 1977.

Dale Spender

Invisible Women: The Schooling Scandal. Writers & Readers Publishing Cooperative Society/Distributed by W.W. Norton, 1983.

Ina Stannard

Mrs. Man. San Francisco: Germain Books, 1977.

Arianna Stassinopoulos

The Female Woman. New York: Random House, 1973.

Peter M. Stearns

Be a Man! Males in Modern Society. New York: Holmes & Meier, Publishers, Inc., 1979.

Nancy Makepeace Tanner

On Becoming Human, Cambridge, NY: Cambridge University Press, 1981.

Carol Tarvis & Carole Offir

The Longest War: Sex Differences in Perspective. New York: Harcourt, Brace, Jovanovich, 1977.

Andrew Tolson

The Limits of Masculinity: Male Identity and Women's Liberation. London: Tavistock, 1977.

Alvin Toffler

"The Fractured Family," chapter 11 in *Future Shock,* New York: Bantam, 1970.

Virginia Tufte & Barbara Myerhoff, Editors

Changing Images of the Family. New Haven, CT: Yale University Press, 1979.

Harold Voth

The Castrated Family. Kansas City: Sheed Andrews and McNeel, Inc., 1977.

James Wagenwood & Peyton Bailey, Producers

Men: A Book for Women. New York: Avon, 1978.

Michelle Wallace

Black Macho and the Myth of the Superwoman. New York: Dial Press, 1979.

Robert H. Walsh, Editor

Marriage and Family 79/80. Annual Editions, Sluice Dock, Guilford, CT: The Dushkin Group, Inc., 1979.

White House Conference on Families

A Summary: Listening to America's Families: Action for the 80's. 330 Independence Avenue S.W., Washington, D.C., 20201, November, 1980.

Elizabeth Friar Williams

Notes of a Feminist Therapist. New York: Laurel Edition/Dell Publishing House, 1976.

Glenn Wilson

The Coolidge Effect: An Evolutionary Account of Human Sexuality. New York: Morrow, 1982.

Gayle Graham Yates

What Women Want: The Ideals of the Movement. Cambridge, MA; Harvard University Press, 1975.

151

Index

The Editors

Bruno Leone received his B.A. (Phi Kappa Phi) from Arizona State University and his M.A. in history from the University of Minnesota. A Woodrow Wilson Fellow (1967), he is currently an instructor at Minneapolis Community College, Minneapolis, Minnesota, where he has taught history, anthropology, and political science. In 1974-1975, he was awarded a Fellowship by the National Endowment for the Humanities to research the intellectual origins of American Democracy. He has authored numerous titles in the *Opposing Viewpoints Series*.

M. Teresa O'Neill received her B.A. from the College of St. Catherine in St. Paul, Minnesota, and her M.A. in American Studies from the University of Minnesota. She is a former magazine editor and teacher of English and Social Studies. She has authored several titles in the *Opposing Viewpoints Series*.